Theme Tests
Teacher Edition
Grade 3

Senior Author
Dr. Roger C. Farr

Chancellor's Professor Emeritus,
Indiana University, Bloomington

Harcourt School Publishers

www.harcourtschool.com

Copyright © by Harcourt, Inc.

All rights reserved. No part of this publication may be reproduced or transmitted in any form or by any means, electronic or mechanical, including photocopy, recording, or any information storage and retrieval system, without permission in writing from the publisher.

Permission is hereby granted to individuals using the corresponding student's textbook or kit as the major vehicle for regular classroom instruction to photocopy Fluency forms from this publication in classroom quantities for instructional use and not for resale. Requests for information on other matters regarding duplication of this work should be addressed to School Permissions and Copyrights, Harcourt, Inc., 6277 Sea Harbor Drive, Orlando, Florida 32887-6777. Fax: 407-345-2418.

HARCOURT and the Harcourt Logo are trademarks of Harcourt, Inc., registered in the United States of America and/or other jurisdictions.

Printed in the United States of America

ISBN 10   0-15-358749-0   ISBN 13   978-0-15-358749-8

9 10   1409   16 15 14 13 12 11 10

Property of Upper Iowa University Waterloo Curriculum Lab

If you have received these materials as examination copies free of charge, Harcourt School Publishers retains title to the materials and they may not be resold. Resale of examination copies is strictly prohibited and is illegal.

Possession of this publication in print format does not entitle users to convert this publication, or any portion of it, into electronic format.

Contents

Overview T3

Administering the Oral Reading Fluency Tests T5

Item Analyses T18

Scoring Responses to Open-Ended Items T30

Scoring Responses to Writing Prompts T37

Assessment Booklets

    Theme 1 Test

    Theme 2 Test

    Theme 3 Test

    Theme 4 Test

    Theme 5 Test

    Theme 6 Test

Overview

Use the *Theme Tests* to monitor students' progress in mastering the skills taught in each theme. The Theme Tests can be given all at once, or you can break up the sections to administer at different times. Use the results of the tests to modify instruction and meet students' individual learning needs.

About the Test Sections

Reading Comprehension
This section assesses the comprehension skills taught in the theme. The skills are integrated so that this test resembles a state test. Each multiple-choice item is worth one point. Each short written response item is worth two points, and each extended written response item is worth four points. See page T30 for the scoring rubric and model top-scoring responses.

Phonics/Spelling
This section assesses students' progress with the phonics/spelling skill or skills in the theme.

Robust Vocabulary
This section assesses robust vocabulary in the theme. Because these questions require students to think deeply about word meanings, both the teacher and students can learn a great deal by discussing students' responses and their reasoning. This not only informs the teacher of students' word knowledge, but also extends instruction and keeps students actively involved with the Robust Vocabulary. It is important to continue to engage students with these words in successive weeks, as true depth of knowledge only results from multiple, meaningful encounters with words. One way to extend this section is to have students write these words in their journals and add stars to show how well they know each word:

☆ I don't know the word.
☆☆ I know the word a little.
☆☆☆ I know the word very well.

Grammar
This section assesses students' progress with the grammar skill in the theme.

Writing to a Prompt
This section assesses students' progress with the writing prompt taught in the Student Writing Model in the theme. See page T37 for directions for the scoring rubric and model responses.

Oral Reading Fluency

Assessing oral reading fluency will help you determine how well a student can apply decoding skills and recognize words quickly. Both narrative and expository passages are provided. The readability has been controlled so that the text is on grade level for students. See page T5 for directions and recording forms.

Scoring and Interpreting the *Theme Tests*

The *Theme Tests* can be scored using the Item Analyses. Follow these steps:
1. Turn to the appropriate Item Analysis on pages T18–T29. (Please see page T5 for scoring and interpreting the Oral Reading Fluency section.)
2. Compare the student's responses, item by item, to the Item Analysis and put a check mark next to each item that is correctly answered. For scoring the open-ended items, please see page T30. For scoring the Writing to a Prompt section, please see page T37.
3. Count the number of correct responses for each test section and write this number on the "Student Score" line on the Performance Summary.
4. Compare the student's total scores for each section to the performance levels provided below the "Student Score" section.

A student who scores at or above the Basic level for each test section is considered competent in that skill area and is probably ready to move forward without additional practice, except for ongoing maintenance.

A student who does not reach the Basic level probably needs additional instruction and/or practice in that particular skill area. Examine the student's scores for each test section and decide whether you should reteach a particular skill, or move forward to the next theme.

Please note: the performance levels are only provided as a guideline for interpreting a student's performance. A *Theme Test* is just one observation of a student's reading and writing behavior. It should be combined with other evidence of a student's progress, such as the teacher's daily observations, student's work samples, and individual conferences. The sum of all this information is more valid and reliable than any single piece of information.

Administering the Oral Reading Fluency Tests

To administer the fluency assessment, use the Oral Reading Fluency Recording Forms. Student copies of the passages are provided with each *Theme Test*. All of the passages are "fresh reads" that students have not read before.

Directions for Administering

1. Explain the task to the student. Tell the student that you want to see how well he or she can read aloud. Inform the student that you will follow along as he or she reads, taking notes. The student may ask about the stopwatch and being timed. Encourage him or her to read at his or her "normal" pace. You don't want the student to speed up and read artificially fast because of the timing.
2. Have the student begin. Use the stopwatch or a second hand to time a one-minute interval as inconspicuously as possible.
3. As the student reads, record reading errors unobtrusively on the Recording Form. Mark mispronunciations, substitutions, omissions of a sound or word, and other errors. *Do not count repetitions or self-corrections as reading errors.*
4. When the stopwatch or second hand reaches the one-minute mark, place a slash mark on the Oral Reading Fluency Recording Form after the last word the student reads. Tell the student to stop reading.

Computing the Fluency Score

1. Total the number of words read by the student in one minute. The row numbers in the right margin will help you determine the number quickly.
2. Count the number of reading errors the student made. Remember, do not count repetitions or self-corrections as reading errors.
3. Subtract the number of reading errors made from the total number of words read correctly. This is the student's oral reading fluency score. Write the words correctly read per minute (WCPM) on the Performance Summary.

Interpreting the Fluency Score

The norms below are based on a study conducted by Hasbrouck and Tindal (2006) in which they established fluency norms for Grades 1 through 8. Look at the WCPM norms below, finding the column that corresponds most closely to the time of year the test was given, and compare the student's score to the norms. Students reading below the 50th percentile may require additional instruction to improve oral reading fluency.

Grade 3 Oral Reading Fluency Norms			
Percentile	Fall	Winter	Spring
25th	44	62	78
50th	71	92	107
75th	99	120	137

Source: Hasbrouck, Jan, and Gerald A. Tindal. 2006. Oral reading fluency norms: A valuable assessment tool for reading teachers. *Reading Teacher* 59 (April), no. 7: 636-644.

Name _____

Oral Reading Fluency

    Today was not a regular day at our school. After 10
lunch all of the classes went to the gym for a special 22
program. 23

    When we walked into the gym, we saw a big stage 34
that was covered with cages of all different shapes and 44
sizes. My friends and I wondered, "What is going on?" 54

    After everyone sat down, our teacher announced 61
that the zoo had brought animals for us to see. The 72
people from the zoo began opening the cages. A 81
woman reached into one cage and pulled out a 90
beautiful green and blue parrot. It squawked loudly 98
and flapped its wings. The next animal we saw was a 109
big brown owl with long claws on its feet. The man 120
holding it was wearing thick gloves to protect his skin. 130

    My favorite animal was a baby alligator. It was sitting 140
so still that I thought it was made out of plastic. But all 153
of a sudden, it snapped its jaws and took everyone by 164
surprise. Today was a really fun day at school, and I will 176
remember it for a long time. 182

Name _____

Theme Test

Theme 1

What do you want to be when you become an adult?	11
Do you want to be an elementary school teacher? How	21
about a doctor or a police officer? No matter what you	32
want to be, you will need an education to make your	43
dream come true. That is why attending school is so	53
important.	54
When you go to school, you learn many skills, such	64
as reading and writing. You also learn about math and	74
science and how to use a computer. Without these	83
skills, you will not be able to get a good job.	94
As you study, you will also learn about yourself and	104
what kind of job you might be good at in the future.	116
You will probably discover that some subjects in school	125
are easier for you than others.	131
Friends are another important part of school. As you	140
work and play with the others in your classroom, you	150
will make many friends. You will learn how to get along	161
with people, which is another skill that you will need	171
when you grow up.	175

Oral Reading Fluency Recording Forms

Oral Reading Fluency

Theme Test
Theme 2

It was the first snowy day of winter. Bob walked	10
outside to shovel his sidewalk. The snow had been	19
falling all night, and it was already about six inches	29
deep. When Bob was about halfway finished with his	38
part of the sidewalk, his arms began to ache.	47
He took a break from shoveling and peered across	56
the street. He waved to his friends who were outside	66
working, too. Then he noticed that the woman	74
everyone in the neighborhood called "Grandma" was	81
outside shoveling her sidewalk alone.	86
"Guys!" he shouted, "Let's pitch in and help	94
Grandma clear away the mess on her sidewalk!"	102
All of Bob's friends rushed to Grandma's part of the	112
sidewalk and began shoveling as quickly as they could.	121
Grandma watched the boys shoveling with tears in	129
her eyes. She was very grateful for their help. "Would	139
you come to my house for hot chocolate when you're	149
finished working?" she asked them. They all agreed.	157
Later that day, they learned that Grandma made the	166
best hot chocolate in town.	171

Name _____

You probably have chores that you do at home. But	10
do you have a responsibility to keep the town where	20
you live running smoothly? If you lived in Nigeria, you	30
probably would.	32
Nigeria is a country in Africa. Most people in Nigeria	42
live in small villages. The people work hard to keep	52
their villages clean and safe. In order to make sure that	63
all of the work is finished, each individual has a job to	75
do. The people of each village are divided into groups	85
by age. Each age group works together to complete its	95
job. Working together makes the job fun.	102
Groups of young children sweep the village and	110
keep it clean. A group of adults is in charge of keeping	122
the water the village uses for drinking and bathing	131
clean. Other groups build houses and roads. The oldest	140
members of the community share stories about the past	149
and give advice to younger people.	155
Because everyone belongs to a group, everyone	162
knows what job to do. The work gets done quickly, and	173
everyone becomes closer to the other members of the	182
community.	183

Oral Reading Fluency

**Theme Test
Theme 3**

Carla raced up the road from the bus stop, hoping	10
that running faster would make her warmer. Her toes	19
were rapidly turning into icicles. In the morning, the	28
breeze had hinted at cool weather, but her red hat, coat,	39
and mittens had kept her warm enough. Now, however,	48
the clouds hung dark and heavy overhead. The cool	57
breeze had turned into an icy wind that cut right	67
through her thick clothing and chilled her aching toes.	76
As Carla pulled the door closed behind her, a gust	86
of wind blew a few snowflakes into the house. She	96
wondered if snow would pile up on the ground during	106
the night. "It is too early in the year for a big storm,"	119
she decided. She put away her coat, hat, and mittens.	129
Then she hurried to thaw out with a cup of hot	140
chocolate.	141
The next morning, the wind whistling around the	149
windows woke Carla up. A thick blanket of white snow	159
covered the ground. Carla gazed at the lacy whiteness,	168
amazed at the change the night had brought. The snow	178
had wrapped the world in white.	184

Name _____

Theme Test
Theme 3

    People, plants, and animals need water to survive.   8
Although water covers much of Earth, most of it is salt   19
water in the oceans and seas. The water in the oceans   30
and seas is much too salty to drink. Salt water also   41
kills many plants that grow on Earth. The water cycle   51
provides the fresh water that living things depend on   60
for life.   62

    The water cycle begins when the sun heats the water   72
in oceans, lakes, and rivers. The heated water changes   81
to a gas, called steam. The steam is lighter than the air   93
so it rises into the atmosphere. High in the sky, the air   105
is colder than the steam, so the steam cools. As it cools,   117
it changes back into water in the form of a cloud.   128

    The cloud grows larger and becomes heavy. When   136
the air can no longer hold the cloud, the water changes   147
to rain, snow, hail, or sleet, and falls to Earth. These are   159
all forms of fresh water. On Earth, some of the water   170
stays in the mountains or on the ground. Some goes   180
into rivers, lakes, and oceans. Then the water cycle   189
starts again.   191

Oral Reading Fluency Recording Forms

Name _____

Oral Reading Fluency

Theme Test
Theme 4

John woke up before sunrise, got dressed, and ate	9
breakfast. Then he searched for his baseball glove. In	18
a few minutes, his uncle would arrive to take him to	29
his first major league baseball game. John had loved	38
baseball for as long as he could remember.	46
When his uncle drove up, John scrambled into the	55
car. After a three-hour drive, John felt excitement rush	65
through him as they arrived at the huge parking lot	75
near the baseball park.	79
John and his uncle located their seats and sat down.	89
The umpire yelled, "Play ball!" and the game began.	98
About halfway through the game, a player hit a ball	108
that appeared to curve directly toward John. He quickly	117
lifted his hand in its baseball glove as high above	127
his head as he could. All of a sudden, he felt his arm	140
bending back, and he almost fell over. He had caught	150
the ball!	152
The rest of the game passed in a blur for John. That	164
night, he fell asleep dreaming about playing catcher in	173
his first big league baseball game!	179

Oral Reading Fluency Recording Forms

Name _____

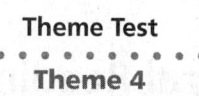

Before Europeans arrived in North America, the 7
Sioux Indian tribe lived on the American plains for 16
hundreds of years. The people of the Sioux tribe have 26
always had many stories to tell about their long history. 36

Long ago, the Sioux told their stories with pictures 45
instead of words. The pictures were painted on the 54
skins of animals that the tribe had hunted. Sioux artists 64
used pictures to tell about events that had happened to 74
the tribe. 76

The Sioux measured a year from one winter to the 86
next, so these picture stories became known as "winter 95
counts." Each picture on the winter count told about 104
one year. As time passed, more and more pictures were 114
added to the winter count. A winter count might tell 124
the stories of wars or big hunts. Later, Sioux winter 134
counts told stories about meeting Europeans. Winter 141
counts help us understand what life was like for the 151
Sioux people many years ago. 156

Could you make a winter count to tell the story 166
of your life? What would it look like? What kinds of 177
stories do you have to tell? 183

Name _____

Oral Reading Fluency

Theme Test
Theme 5

I live on the third floor of a five-story apartment	11
building with my mom, dad, and little sister Clara.	20
Many friendly people live in our building. Mrs.	28
Morton lives next door with her prize-winning	36
poodle. Sometimes we pass them in the elevator or	45
on the sidewalk. Dad says the dog keeps Mrs. Morton	55
company. I'd like to have a dog, too, but mom says	66
dogs are too much work. Besides, she says, I have Clara	77
to keep me company.	81
When I'm not with Clara, I'm with my best friend	91
Lin. She lives on the first floor. Lin's family is from	102
China. Each morning, I leave my apartment and	110
ride the elevator to the first floor where Lin waits for	121
me. We walk to the bus stop, chatting and giggling.	131
Sometimes after school, Lin and I sit at the big table	142
in her living room and finish our homework. On	151
Saturdays, we like to play board games. I know how	161
lucky I am to have a friend in the building!	171
My mom and dad have friends in the building, too.	181
Mr. and Mrs. Sanchez live upstairs. Sometimes they	189
come downstairs and play cards with my parents. Clara	198
and I can hear them laughing even after we go to bed.	210
We all laugh a lot in our building full of friends.	221

Oral Reading Fluency Recording Forms

Name _____

Theme Test
Theme 5

When you visit a park, do you see broken bottles on	11
the ground or dirty plastic bags? Do you notice empty	21
candy boxes and crushed cans when you look down at	31
the sidewalk? If you do, you understand how garbage	40
can spoil the neighborhoods we live in, if it isn't picked	51
up and thrown away.	55
Garbage can be dangerous, if it is not in the right	66
place. If there is broken glass on the ground at a park,	78
someone could get cut by the glass while playing.	87
Garbage is not safe for nature. Plastic bottles on grass	97
will keep it from growing. Animals such as birds,	106
squirrels, and rabbits can become tangled in plastic	114
strings so that they can't move. They might be injured	124
or die.	126
Each person who lives in a neighborhood should	134
keep the neighborhood clean. If everyone picked up	142
one piece of garbage each day, just imagine how much	152
cleaner our neighborhoods would be. You can make a	161
difference. The next time you see a piece of trash on the	173
ground, pick it up and help make your neighborhood a	183
nicer place.	185

Oral Reading Fluency Recording Forms   T15

Name _____

Theme Test
Theme 6

Oral Reading Fluency

Katie Clare is a nine-year-old detective. She solves	10
mysteries that are very old. How does she do it?	20
Katie is a fossil collector, or "rock hound." Almost	29
every weekend, Katie and her parents go fossil hunting.	38
Katie has never found a dinosaur fossil. The fossils	47
she finds are just as interesting, though. When she	56
finds one, Katie carefully chips at the rock around it	66
with her hammer. Once the fossil is out, she wraps it	77
carefully in newspaper. Then she puts it in her bag.	87
Some of the things Katie finds are too difficult to	97
collect. They might be damaged if she tried to remove	107
them from the rock. Katie places soft paper over the	117
rock and then rubs charcoal on the paper to make a	128
picture of the leaf or shell that is buried in the rock.	140
When Katie gets home, she takes out her fossils and	150
her rubbings. She uses her fossil book to look up the	161
names and ages of her plant and animal fossils. Then	171
she sorts the rocks carefully into little boxes. These	180
boxes make up her collection.	185

Oral Reading Fluency Recording Forms

Have you ever had an idea for a new invention? People are always coming up with new ideas, but very few people have the skill to make their inventions. That is why Beulah Henry is so special.

Beulah Henry was born in 1887. She is known to have had 49 inventions during her life. Some people believe she had ideas for more than 100 inventions.

Many of Beulah Henry's inventions were for children. She invented a kind of sponge that made bath time more fun. She also invented learning games.

Beulah Henry came up with many inventions to make housework easier. She made new kinds of sewing machines and a new kind of can opener.

The best known of Beulah Henry's inventions was a new kind of umbrella. It was made with snaps. People could snap different colored fabrics onto the umbrella to match their clothing. Many people wanted to buy these umbrellas. They were sold all over the country.

Beulah Henry died in 1973. In her long life, she came up with more inventions than almost any other inventor of her time.

Item Analysis: Theme 1 Test

Item	Correct Answer	Skill	Cognitive Complexity*	Webb's Depth of Knowledge**
		Reading Comprehension		
1	C	Locate Information	Low	Level 1
2	F	Locate Information	Moderate	Level 2
3	D	Alphabetical Order	Low	Level 1
4	G	Locate Information	Low	Level 1
5	A	Use a Dictionary	Low	Level 1
6	I	Locate Information	Moderate	Level 2
7	C	Characters and Setting	Moderate	Level 2
8	F	Locate Information	Moderate	Level 2
9	D	Locate Information	Low	Level 1
10	H	Alphabetical Order	Low	Level 1
11	C	Characters and Setting	Moderate	Level 2
12	H	Characters and Setting	High	Level 3
13	*	Characters and Setting	High	Level 3

* See page T30 for the scoring rubric and model top-scoring responses.

Item	Correct Answer	Skill	Cognitive Complexity*	Webb's Depth of Knowledge**
14	C	Characters and Setting	Moderate	Level 2
15	I	Locate Information	Low	Level 1
16	A	Characters and Setting	Moderate	Level 2
17	H	Use a Dictionary	Moderate	Level 2
18	A	Characters and Setting	Moderate	Level 2
19	F	Alphabetical Order	Low	Level 1
20	*	Characters and Setting	High	Level 3

* See page T30 for the scoring rubric and model top-scoring responses.

Item	Correct Answer	Skill	Cognitive Complexity*	Webb's Depth of Knowledge**
		Phonics/Spelling		
21	A	Short Vowels /a/a, /e/e, /i/i, /o/o, /u/u	NA	—
22	H	Short Vowels /a/a, /e/e, /i/i, /o/o, /u/u	—	—
23	A	Short Vowels /a/a, /e/e, /i/i, /o/o, /u/u	—	—
24	G	Short Vowels /a/a, /e/e, /i/i, /o/o, /u/u	—	—
25	D	Short Vowels /a/a, /e/e, /i/i, /o/o, /u/u	—	—
26	G	Vowel Digraphs ee, ea, ai, ay, oa, ow	—	—
27	B	Vowel Digraphs ee, ea, ai, ay, oa, ow	—	—
28	F	Vowel Digraphs ee, ea, ai, ay, oa, ow	—	—
29	B	Vowel Digraphs ee, ea, ai, ay, oa, ow	—	—
30	H	Root Word + Ending -ed, -ing	—	—
31	B	Root Word + Ending -ed, -ing	—	—
32	H	Root Word + Ending -ed, -ing	—	—
33	C	Plurals -s, -es	—	—
34	G	Plurals -s, -es	—	—
35	C	Plurals -s, -es	—	—

Item Analysis: Theme 1 Test

		Robust Vocabulary		
Item	Correct Answer	Skill	Cognitive Complexity	Webb's Depth of Knowledge
36	G	Robust Vocabulary	NA	—
37	D	Robust Vocabulary	—	—
38	H	Robust Vocabulary	—	—
39	A	Robust Vocabulary	—	—
40	H	Robust Vocabulary	—	—
41	D	Robust Vocabulary	—	—
42	F	Robust Vocabulary	—	—
43	B	Robust Vocabulary	—	—
44	I	Robust Vocabulary	—	—
45	D	Robust Vocabulary	—	—
Grammar				
46	F	Sentences; Statements and Questions	NA	—
47	D	Sentences; Statements and Questions	—	—
48	F	Commands and Exclamations	—	—
49	D	Commands and Exclamations	—	—
50	F	Compound Subjects and Predicates	—	—
51	B	Compound Subjects and Predicates	—	—
52	G	Sentences; Statements and Questions	—	—
53	D	Sentences; Statements and Questions	—	—
54	H	Compound Subjects and Predicates	—	—
55	B	Compound Subjects and Predicates	—	—
Writing to a Prompt				
	See page T37 for scoring rubric and model responses.		High (six points possible)	Level 3
Oral Reading Fluency				
	See page T5 for Oral Reading Fluency Norms.			

NA: not applicable

Item Analysis: Theme 1 Test

Item Analysis: Theme 2 Test

		Reading Comprehension		
Item	Correct Answer	Skill	Cognitive Complexity	Webb's Depth of Knowledge
1	C	Synonyms and Antonyms	Moderate	Level 2
2	G	Fact and Opinion	Moderate	Level 2
3	D	Use Reference Sources	Moderate	Level 2
4	I	Main Idea and Details	Low	Level 1
5	C	Fact and Opinion	Moderate	Level 2
6	G	Use Reference Sources	Moderate	Level 2
7	*	Main Idea and Details	High	Level 3
		* See page T30 for the scoring rubric and model top-scoring responses.		
8	B	Synonyms and Antonyms	Moderate	Level 2
9	G	Main Idea and Details	Moderate	Level 2
10	C	Main Idea and Details	Low	Level 1
11	H	Fact and Opinion	Moderate	Level 2
12	B	Use Reference Sources	Moderate	Level 2
13	*	Characters and Setting	High	Level 3
		* See page T30 for the scoring rubric and model top-scoring responses.		
14	I	Main Idea and Details	Moderate	Level 2
15	D	Main Idea and Details	Moderate	Level 2
16	I	Use Reference Sources	Moderate	Level 2
17	C	Synonyms and Antonyms	High	Level 3
18	F	Fact and Opinion	Moderate	Level 2
19	D	Main Idea and Details	Low	Level 1
20	F	Synonyms and Antonyms	Moderate	Level 2
		Phonics/Spelling		
21	B	Compound Words	NA	—
22	F	Compound Words	—	—
23	D	Compound Words	—	—
24	H	Compound Words	—	—
25	B	Consonant Digraphs /ch/*ch*, tch; /sh/*sh*, *ch*; /(h)w/*wh*	—	—
26	F	Consonant Digraphs /ch/*ch*, tch; /sh/*sh*, *ch*; /(h)w/*wh*	—	—
27	C	Diphthongs /ou/*ou, ow*, /oi/ *oi, oy*	—	—
28	H	Diphthongs /ou/*ou, ow*, /oi/ *oi, oy*	—	—
29	C	Diphthongs /ou/*ou, ow*, /oi/ *oi, oy*	—	—
30	I	Consonant Digraphs /ch/*ch*, tch; /sh/*sh*, *ch*; /(h)w/*wh*	—	—
31	B	Diphthongs /ou/*ou, ow*, /oi/ *oi, oy*	—	—
32	H	Consonant Digraphs /ch/*ch*, tch; /sh/*sh*, *ch*; /(h)w/*wh*	—	—
33	D	Consonant Blends: *str, scr, spr*	—	—
34	H	Consonant Blends: *str, scr, spr*	—	—
35	A	Consonant Blends: *str, scr, spr*	—	—

Item Analysis: Theme 2 Test

Item	Correct Answer	Skill	Cognitive Complexity	Webb's Depth of Knowledge
	Robust Vocabulary			
36	G	Robust Vocabulary	NA	—
37	C	Robust Vocabulary	—	—
38	H	Robust Vocabulary	—	—
39	D	Robust Vocabulary	—	—
40	F	Robust Vocabulary	—	—
41	B	Robust Vocabulary	—	—
42	F	Robust Vocabulary	—	—
43	A	Robust Vocabulary	—	—
44	I	Robust Vocabulary	—	—
45	B	Robust Vocabulary	—	—
	Grammar			
46	H	Simple and Compound Sentences	NA	—
47	B	Simple and Compound Sentences	—	—
48	I	Simple and Compound Sentences	—	—
49	C	Common and Proper Nouns	—	—
50	H	Common and Proper Nouns	—	—
51	B	Abbreviations	—	—
52	F	Abbreviations	—	—
53	B	Singular and Plural Nouns	—	—
54	G	Singular and Plural Nouns	—	—
55	D	Singular and Plural Nouns	—	—
	Writing to a Prompt			
colspan="3"	See page T37 for scoring rubric and model responses.	High (six points possible)	Level 3
	Oral Reading Fluency			
	See page T5 for Oral Reading Fluency Norms.			

Item Analysis: Theme 2 Test

Item Analysis: Theme 3 Test

Reading Comprehension				
Item	Correct Answer	Skill	Cognitive Complexity	Webb's Depth of Knowledge
1	B	Plot	Moderate	Level 2
2	F	Use Context Clues	Moderate	Level 2
3	D	Plot	High	Level 3
4	I	Locate Information	Low	Level 1
5	A	Author's Purpose	High	Level 3
6	*	Author's Purpose	High	Level 3
* See page T30 for the scoring rubric and model top-scoring responses.				
7	G	Main Idea and Details	Moderate	Level 2
8	A	Author's Purpose	Moderate	Level 2
9	H	Main Idea and Details	High	Level 3
10	B	Use Graphic Aids	Moderate	Level 2
11	H	Use Graphic Aids	Low	Level 1
12	C	Use Graphic Aids	High	Level 3
13	*	Main Idea and Details	High	Level 3
* See page T30 for the scoring rubric and model top-scoring responses.				
14	G	Plot	Low	Level 1
15	D	Use Context Clues	Moderate	Level 2
16	H	Author's Purpose	High	Level 3
17	A	Characters and Setting	Moderate	Level 2
18	H	Plot	Low	Level 1
19	C	Plot	Low	Level 1
20	I	Plot	Low	Level 1
Phonics/Spelling				
21	A	C-*le* Syllable	NA	—
22	G	C-*le* Syllable	—	—
23	B	C-*le* Syllable	—	—
24	H	C-*le* Syllable	—	—
25	A	Consonant Digraphs /n/ *kn, gn*; /r/ *wr*; /f/ *gh*	—	—
26	G	Consonant Digraphs /n/ *kn, gn*; /r/ *wr*; /f/ *gh*	—	—
27	D	Consonant Digraphs /n/ *kn, gn*; /r/ *wr*; /f/ *gh*	—	—
28	H	Consonant Digraphs /n/ *kn, gn*; /r/ *wr*; /f/ *gh*	—	—
29	D	Consonants /s/ *c*; /j/ *g, dge*	—	—
30	F	Consonants /s/ *c*; /j/ *g, dge*	—	—
31	C	Consonants /s/ *c*; /j/ *g, dge*	—	—
32	H	V/CV and VC/V Syllable Patterns	—	—
33	A	V/CV and VC/V Syllable Patterns	—	—
34	F	V/CV and VC/V Syllable Patterns	—	—
35	C	V/CV and VC/V Syllable Patterns	—	—

Item Analysis: Theme 3 Test

© Harcourt • Grade 3

Robust Vocabulary				
Item	Correct Answer	Skill	Cognitive Complexity	Webb's Depth of Knowledge
36	G	Robust Vocabulary	NA	—
37	A	Robust Vocabulary	—	—
38	H	Robust Vocabulary	—	—
39	A	Robust Vocabulary	—	—
40	G	Robust Vocabulary	—	—
41	D	Robust Vocabulary	—	—
42	I	Robust Vocabulary	—	—
43	D	Robust Vocabulary	—	—
44	H	Robust Vocabulary	—	—
45	D	Robust Vocabulary	—	—
Grammar				
46	F	Singular And Plural Pronouns	NA	—
47	B	Possessive Nouns	—	—
48	I	Possessive Nouns	—	—
49	B	Pronoun-Antecedent Agreement	—	—
50	I	Pronoun-Antecedent Agreement	—	—
51	B	Subject and Object Pronouns	—	—
52	H	Subject and Object Pronouns	—	—
53	B	Subject and Object Pronouns	—	—
54	I	Possessive Nouns	—	—
55	B	Pronoun-Antecedent Agreement	—	—
Writing to a Prompt				
See page T37 for scoring rubric and model responses.			High (six points possible)	Level 3
Oral Reading Fluency				
See page T5 for Oral Reading Fluency Norms.				

Item Analysis: Theme 3 Test

Item Analysis: Theme 4 Test

Reading Comprehension				
Item	Correct Answer	Skill	Cognitive Complexity	Webb's Depth of Knowledge
1	B	Compare and Contrast	Moderate	Level 2
2	G	Compare and Contrast	High	Level 3
3	C	Theme	High	Level 3
4	H	Follow Directions	Low	Level 1
5	B	Follow Directions	Low	Level 1
6	G	Follow Directions	Low	Level 1
7	D	Use Reference Sources	Moderate	Level 2
8	F	Theme	Moderate	Level 2
9	C	Compare and Contrast	Moderate	Level 2
10	F	Characters and Setting	Low	Level 1
11	C	Prefixes and Suffixes	Low	Level 1
12	I	Prefixes and Suffixes	Low	Level 1
13	B	Use Reference Sources	Moderate	Level 2
14	*	Compare and Contrast	High	Level 3
* See page T30 for the scoring rubric and model top-scoring responses.				
15	I	Locate Information	Moderate	Level 2
16	A	Prefixes and Suffixes	Moderate	Level 2
17	H	Theme	High	Level 3
18	A	Main Idea and Details	Moderate	Level 2
19	F	Fact and Opinion	Moderate	Level 2
20	*	Compare and Contrast	High	Level 3
* See page T30 for the scoring rubric and model top-scoring responses.				
Phonics/Spelling				
21	D	r-Controlled Vowels: /ôr/or, ore, our, oar, ar	NA	—
22	I	r-Controlled Vowels: /ôr/or, ore, our, oar, ar	—	—
23	C	r-Controlled Vowels: /ôr/or, ore, our, oar, ar	—	—
24	G	r-Controlled Vowels: /ôr/or, ore, our, oar, ar	—	—
25	D	r-Controlled Vowels: /ûr/ er, ir, ur, or, ear	—	—
26	H	r-Controlled Vowels: /ûr/ er, ir, ur, or, ear	—	—
27	C	r-Controlled Vowels: /ûr/ er, ir, ur, or, ear	—	—
28	F	r-Controlled Vowels: /ûr/ er, ir, ur, or, ear	—	—
29	C	Suffixes: -er, -est, -ly, -ful	—	—
30	I	Suffixes: -er, -est, -ly, -ful	—	—
31	C	Suffixes: -er, -est, -ly, -ful	—	—
32	G	Suffixes: -er, -est, -ly, -ful	—	—
33	B	Prefixes: un-, re-, dis-	—	—
34	I	Prefixes: un-, re-, dis-	—	—
35	C	Prefixes: un-, re-, dis-	—	—

Item Analysis: Theme 4 Test

Robust Vocabulary				
Item	Correct Answer	Skill	Cognitive Complexity	Webb's Depth of Knowledge
36	G	Robust Vocabulary	NA	—
37	D	Robust Vocabulary	—	—
38	F	Robust Vocabulary	—	—
39	A	Robust Vocabulary	—	—
40	F	Robust Vocabulary	—	—
41	D	Robust Vocabulary	—	—
42	F	Robust Vocabulary	—	—
43	A	Robust Vocabulary	—	—
44	H	Robust Vocabulary	—	—
45	D	Robust Vocabulary	—	—
Grammar				
46	I	Adjectives	NA	—
47	D	Comparing Adjectives	—	—
48	F	Comparing Adjectives	—	—
49	C	Comparing Adjectives	—	—
50	G	Articles	—	—
51	B	Action Verbs	—	—
52	I	Action Verbs	—	—
53	B	Articles	—	—
54	I	Adjectives	—	—
55	B	Articles	—	—
Writing to a Prompt				
See page T37 for scoring rubric and model responses.			High (six points possible)	Level 3
Oral Reading Fluency				
See page T5 for Oral Reading Fluency Norms.				

Item Analysis: Theme 4 Test

Item Analysis: Theme 5 Test

Reading Comprehension				
Item	Correct Answer	Skill	Cognitive Complexity	Webb's Depth of Knowledge
1	B	Cause and Effect	Moderate	Level 2
2	I	Sequence	Moderate	Level 2
3	B	Use Reference Sources	Low	Level 1
4	G	Author's Message	Moderate	Level 2
5	D	Synonyms and Antonyms	Moderate	Level 2
6	I	Homophones	Moderate	Level 2
7	*	Cause and Effect	High	Level 3
* See page T30 for the scoring rubric and model top-scoring responses.				
8	D	Use Context Clues	Low	Level 1
9	I	Characters and Setting	Moderate	Level 2
10	A	Sequence	Low	Level 1
11	G	Author's Message	Moderate	Level 2
12	B	Cause and Effect	Moderate	Level 2
13	*	Cause and Effect	High	Level 3
* See page T30 for the scoring rubric and model top-scoring responses.				
14	F	Homophones	Moderate	Level 2
15	C	Locate Information	Low	Level 1
16	I	Cause and Effect	Moderate	Level 2
17	A	Sequence	Low	Level 1
18	H	Author's Message	Moderate	Level 2
19	C	Homophones	Moderate	Level 2
20	H	Plot	Moderate	Level 2
Phonics/Spelling				
21	C	Vowel Variants: /oo/ oo, ew, ue, ui; /o͝o/o͞o/	NA	—
22	G	Vowel Variants: /oo/ oo, ew, ue, ui; /o͝o/o͞o/	—	—
23	D	Vowel Variants: /oo/ oo, ew, ue, ui; /o͝o/o͞o/	—	—
24	H	Vowel Variants: /oo/ oo, ew, ue, ui; /o͝o/o͞o/	—	—
25	C	Vowel Variant: /ô/ o, au (gh), aw, a (l), ough	—	—
26	G	Vowel Variant: /ô/o, au(gh), aw, a(l), ough	—	—
27	B	Vowel Variant: /ô/o, au(gh), aw, a(l), ough	—	—
28	G	Vowel Variant: /ô/o, au(gh), aw, a(l), ough	—	—
29	B	Prefixes pre-, mis-, in-	—	—
30	H	Prefixes pre-, mis-, in-	—	—
31	D	Prefixes pre-, mis-, in-	—	—
32	H	Schwa /ə/	—	—
33	A	Schwa /ə/	—	—
34	H	Schwa /ə/	—	—
35	D	Schwa /ə/	—	—

		Robust Vocabulary		
Item	Correct Answer	Skill	Cognitive Complexity	Webb's Depth of Knowledge
36	H	Robust Vocabulary	NA	—
37	B	Robust Vocabulary	—	—
38	I	Robust Vocabulary	—	—
39	A	Robust Vocabulary	—	—
40	I	Robust Vocabulary	—	—
41	A	Robust Vocabulary	—	—
42	G	Robust Vocabulary	—	—
43	D	Robust Vocabulary	—	—
44	G	Robust Vocabulary	—	—
45	B	Robust Vocabulary	—	—
		Grammar		
46	G	The Verb *Be*	NA	—
47	C	Main and Helping Verbs	—	—
48	G	Main and Helping Verbs	—	—
49	A	Present-Tense Verbs	—	—
50	H	Past-Tense and Future-Tense Verbs	—	—
51	D	Past-Tense and Future-Tense Verbs	—	—
52	H	Main and Helping Verbs	—	—
53	A	Past-Tense and Future-Tense Verbs	—	—
54	G	The Verb *Be*	—	—
55	A	Present-Tense Verbs	—	—
		Writing to a Prompt		
		See page T37 for scoring rubric and model responses.	High (six points possible)	Level 3
		Oral Reading Fluency		
		See page T5 for Oral Reading Fluency Norms.		

Item Analysis: Theme 5 Test

Item Analysis: Theme 6 Test

		Reading Comprehension		
Item	Correct Answer	Skill	Cognitive Complexity	Webb's Depth of Knowledge
1	C	Make Inferences	Moderate	Level 2
2	H	Make Predictions	High	Level 3
3	B	Multiple-Meaning Words	Low	Level 1
4	G	Main Idea and Details	Low	Level 1
5	A	Compare and Contrast	Moderate	Level 2
6	G	Homographs	Moderate	Level 2
7	C	Use Reference Sources	Low	Level 1
8	I	Fact And Opinion	Low	Level 1
9	C	Sequence	Low	Level 1
10	F	Multiple-Meaning Words	Moderate	Level 2
11	A	Make Inferences	Moderate	Level 2
12	I	Characters and Setting	Moderate	Level 2
13	*	Make Predictions	High	Level 3
* See page T30 for the scoring rubric and model top-scoring responses.				
14	C	Author's Purpose	Moderate	Level 2
15	G	Make Inferences	High	Level 3
16	D	Make Predictions	High	Level 3
17	I	Multiple-Meaning Words	Low	Level 1
18	C	Homographs	Moderate	Level 2
19	F	Homographs	Moderate	Level 2
20	*	Main Idea and Details	Moderate	Level 2
* See page T30 for the scoring rubric and model top-scoring responses.				
Phonics/Spelling				
21	D	Suffixes *-tion, -sion*	NA	—
22	G	Suffixes *-tion, -sion*	—	—
23	D	Suffixes *-tion, -sion*	—	—
24	H	Suffixes *-able, -ible, -less, -ous*	—	—
25	A	Suffixes *-able, -ible, -less, -ous*	—	—
26	G	Suffixes *-able, -ible, -less, -ous*	—	—
27	D	Suffixes *-able, -ible, -less, -ous*	—	—
28	F	Prefixes *bi-, non-, over-*	—	—
29	C	Prefixes *bi-, non-, over-*	—	—
30	I	Prefixes *bi-, non-, over-*	—	—
31	D	Suffixes *-able, -ible, -less, -ous*	—	—
32	G	V/V Syllable Pattern	—	—
33	B	V/V Syllable Pattern	—	—
34	G	V/V Syllable Pattern	—	—
35	B	V/V Syllable Pattern	—	—

Item Analysis: Theme 6 Test

Robust Vocabulary				
Item	Correct Answer	Skill	Cognitive Complexity	Webb's Depth of Knowledge
36	F	Robust Vocabulary	NA	—
37	B	Robust Vocabulary	—	—
38	I	Robust Vocabulary	—	—
39	C	Robust Vocabulary	—	—
40	G	Robust Vocabulary	—	—
41	B	Robust Vocabulary	—	—
42	G	Robust Vocabulary	—	—
43	D	Robust Vocabulary	—	—
44	G	Robust Vocabulary	—	—
45	D	Robust Vocabulary	—	—
Grammar				
46	F	Irregular Verbs	NA	—
47	A	Irregular Verbs	—	—
48	G	Irregular Verbs	—	—
49	D	Adverbs	—	—
50	I	Adverbs	—	—
51	B	Punctuation Roundup	—	—
52	H	Contractions	—	—
53	A	Contractions	—	—
54	G	Punctuation Roundup	—	—
55	C	Punctuation Roundup	—	—
Writing to a Prompt				
See page T37 for scoring rubric and model responses.			High (six points possible)	Level 3
Oral Reading Fluency				
See page T5 for Oral Reading Fluency Norms.				

* The cognitive complexity of an item is a measure of the level of thinking required of the student.

** Webb's Depth of Knowledge refers to the level of knowledge the item requires of the student. For more information see: Webb, N.L., 1999, Alignment Between Standards and Assessment, University of Wisconsin Center for Educational Research.

Item Analysis: Theme 6 Test

Scoring Responses to Open-Ended Items

Use the rubrics below to score the open-ended items found in the Reading Comprehension section of the *Theme Tests*.

Short Written Response Rubric		
2 points	• Shows good attention to the task • Clearly based on the text the student read • Includes adequate support or examples • Accurate and complete	READ THINK EXPLAIN
1 point	• Shows some attention to the task • Somewhat based on the text the student read • Includes some support or examples • Contains some inaccurate or incomplete details	
0 points	• Shows no attention to the task • Not clearly based on the text the student read • Lacks support or examples • Inaccurate and incomplete	

Extended Written Response Rubric		
4 points	• Shows complete awareness of the task • Clearly based on the text the student read • Includes effective support or examples • Accurate and complete	READ THINK EXPLAIN
3 points	• Shows a general attention to the task • Generally based on the text the student read • Includes mostly adequate support or examples • Mostly accurate and complete	
2 points	• Shows some attention to the task • Somewhat based on the text the student read • Some support or examples are inadequate • May contain some inaccuracies or be partially incomplete	
1 point	• Shows minimal attention to the task • Minimally based on the text the student read • Includes little support or examples • Contains inaccurate or incomplete details	
0 points	• Shows no attention to the task • Not clearly based on the text the student read • Lacks support or examples • Inaccurate and incomplete	

Scoring Responses to Open-Ended Items

Model Responses to Open-Ended Items

Below are top-scoring answers for each of the open-ended items found in the Reading Comprehension section of the *Theme Tests*.

Theme 1 Test

13. Explain two things you learn about Sam and his family from the story. Use details and information from the story to support your answer.

    Model two-point response: Sam's family is very busy. Everyone is doing something at the last minute. They all seem like nice people. Sam's dad tries to help him, and his mom smiles instead of getting upset with Sam.

20. How does Jacob's attitude toward his homework and his home change? Use details and information from the story to support your answer.

    Model four-point response: At the beginning of the story, Jacob does not think that his homework assignment is fair. He glares out the window of the school bus because he is so angry about it. He thinks that students who live in the city will have an easy time doing the homework because there are so many noises around them. He thinks that he will not be able to do the homework because he lives on a farm. He thinks that farms are quiet places where nothing exciting happens. Since Jacob doesn't think he can do the assignment on the farm, he doesn't notice all of the noises that he hears there. Finally, Jacob hears so many sounds at once that he yells "QUIET!" Then he realizes what he has been missing. There are many sounds on a farm. There are sounds in the house and in the yard. There are also many animal sounds. Once Jacob realizes this, he runs inside to do his homework. Now he seems excited to do the homework. He also has realized what a great home he has.

Theme 2 Test

7. The article tells about two problems monarch butterflies face. Choose one of these problems and describe a possible solution. Use information and details from the article to support your answer.

   Model four-point response: One of the problems facing the monarch butterfly is that people are cutting down trees. These trees are home to butterflies during the winter. Butterflies need these homes for protection. People should be careful not to cut down too many trees. They should pay attention to where butterflies live and make sure that they leave enough trees for the butterflies to have homes. This way, people will still be able to have wood for building, and monarch butterflies will be able to have winter homes.

13. This story has two characters, Antonio and Anita. What two characteristics do Antonio and Anita share? Use information and details from the story to support your answer.

    Model two-point response: In the story, Antonio and Anita are both characters who are caring and hard-working. They want to clean up the neighborhood park, which shows that they care about their community. Antonio and Anita are hard-working: in order to accomplish their goal, they are willing to work and to persuade others to help them.

Model Responses to Open-Ended Items

Theme 3 Test

6. What does the author want the reader to know about friendship? Use details and information from the story to explain your answer.

   Model four-point response: The author wants the reader to understand that friendship is important, but that it isn't always easy. In order to show that friendship is important, the author describes the friendship that Rita and Paula had before the election. They ate lunch together at school and Rita would call Paula at night to talk about their day at school. The author also points out that friends are good companions for lunchtime. The author also shows that friendship isn't always easy. Although Rita and Paula are best friends, they both want to be president. It is hard for Rita to get over her jealousy when Paula wins the election. She feels disappointed because she wanted to be president. Although the two girls try to be friends, it isn't as easy as it was before. Both girls end up spending time with other friends. They will have to work hard to become best friends again.

13. The article explains how language has changed with the invention and use of computers. Using information from the article, choose one word, and explain its different meanings.

    Model two-point response: The word *crash* has developed new meanings over time. People used to think of the loud sound that objects make when they fall. Then, as people began to drive cars, they started to use the word to refer to a car accident. Now that we have computers, it is common to use the word to mean when a computer stops working.

Model Responses to Open-Ended Items

Theme 4 Test

14. Write about how dinner at Jenna's house changes. Compare what you think dinner was like before Monday night to what it is like after. Use details and information from the story to explain your answer.

Model four-point response: Before Monday night, dinner at Jenna's house was probably not very exciting. Jenna did not like to set the table. She thought that it was boring. The family probably didn't have a lot of fun at dinner. Everyone in the family seems to have been ready for a change. That is why Jenna's plans work out so well. After Monday night, the family had a lot more fun at dinner. Jenna didn't mind setting the table. She used her imagination to make the job fun. The family enjoyed seeing what she had planned. They enjoyed acting out the creative ideas that Jenna had come up with. They smiled and laughed. They really seemed to enjoy eating together.

20. Tell ONE way Mary Cassatt was LIKE other Impressionists. Tell ONE way Mary Cassatt was DIFFERENT from other impressionists.

Model two-point response: One thing Mary Cassatt had in common with other Impressionist painters is that she studied art in Paris. She also painted everyday scenes. However, unlike other Impressionist artists, Mary Cassatt was an American art student in Paris, and she was a woman.

Model Responses to Open-Ended Items

Theme 5 Test

7. The article explains that each elephant in a herd plays an important role. Choose ONE of these roles, and explain what effect this role has on the herd.

   Model two-point response: Babysitters play an important role in elephant herds. Without them, mother elephants would not be able to produce enough milk to feed their babies. The babysitters allow mother elephants to find and eat enough food so that they can make enough milk for their babies. Baby elephants are an important part of the herd. They are the herd's future. The babysitters make sure that the herd will continue to grow.

13. Explain how the story shows that good things come from helping others. Use details and information from the story to explain your answer.

    Model four-point response: The story shows that good things come from helping others. James helps others by taking all of the old toys that he doesn't use any more to Anna's house. Anna will give these toys to other children who would like to play with them. Another good thing that comes from helping others is that James gets the skateboard that he wanted. James does a good thing and gives his toys to Anna even though she doesn't have a skateboard to give him in return. The next day, James gets a message that Anna has found him a skateboard. Because he did a good deed, he not only helped other kids find the toys they wanted, but he earned the skateboard that he wanted.

Model Responses to Open-Ended Items

Theme 6 Test

13. What would have MOST LIKELY happened if Mole hadn't landed in the puddle? Use details and information from the story to support your answer.

   Model two-point response: If Mole hadn't landed in the puddle, he probably would have kept trying to pull down the moon. Before he climbed the tree and fell into the puddle, Mole tried jumping at the moon, poking and throwing things at the moon. He was determined to reach it. He only stopped because he thought the moon was broken. If he hadn't seen the moon's reflection, he probably would have kept coming up with different ways to try to reach it.

20. Write about Charles Lindbergh's important flight. Why was it so important? How does the author help you understand how important the flight was? Use details and information from the story to explain your answer.

   Model four-point response: Airplanes were still a brand new invention when Charles Lindbergh flew across the Atlantic Ocean, and no one had ever flown across the Atlantic in an airplane before. The author writes that someone was willing to offer a large reward to the pilot who could fly across the Atlantic. The author also tells us that one hundred thousand people were waiting for Lindbergh in Paris. This shows how special and important his flight was. The author says at the end of the article that Lindbergh was a hero, a special title for someone who does a very important thing.

Model Responses to Open-Ended Items

Scoring Responses to Writing Prompts

Use the rubric below to score students' responses to the writing prompts on the *Theme Tests*.

	Score of 6	Score of 5	Score of 4	Score of 3	Score of 2	Score of 1
Focus	The writing is completely focused on the topic and has a clear purpose.	The writing is focused on the topic and purpose.	The writing is generally focused on the topic and purpose.	The writing is somewhat focused on the topic and purpose.	The writing is related to the topic but does not have a clear focus.	The writing is not focused on the topic and purpose.
Organization	The ideas in the writing are well-organized and presented in logical order. The paper seems complete to the reader.	The organization of the writing is mostly clear. The paper seems complete.	The organization is mostly clear, but the writing may seem unfinished.	The writing is somewhat organized, but seems unfinished.	There is little organization to the writing.	There is no organization to the writing.
Support	The writing has strong, specific details. The word choices are clear and fresh.	The writing has strong, specific details and clear word choices.	The writing has supporting details and some variety in word choice.	The writing has few supporting details. It needs more variety in word choice.	The writing uses few supporting details and very little variety in word choice.	There are few or no supporting details. The word choices are unclear.
Conventions	The writer uses a variety of sentences. There are few or no errors in grammar, spelling, punctuation, and capitalization.	The writer uses a variety of sentences. There are a few errors in grammar, spelling, punctuation, and capitalization.	The writer uses some variety in sentences. There are a few errors in grammar, spelling, punctuation, and capitalization.	The writer uses simple sentences. There are some errors in grammar, spelling, punctuation, and capitalization.	The writer uses simple sentences. There are many errors in grammar, spelling, punctuation, and capitalization.	The writer uses unclear sentences. There are many errors in grammar, spelling, punctuation, and capitalization.

Model Responses to Writing Prompts

Theme 1 Writing Prompt

Everyone has learned something that is important.

Think about a time you learned something important.

Now write a story about a time when you learned something important.

Score 6

The story is very engaging because of the solid organization, supporting details, and clever word choice ("...in a split second I dashed out of the room so quick I looked like I was faster than lightning."). Both the mature command of language and a variety of sentence structures add to its integrity. Minor spelling errors do not detract from meaning.

One day when I was 4 my dad and mom told me "Do not do anything dangerous or play with fire." I did as I was told. Then 5 years passed and I was being stupid as could be.

That day my dad told me to clean my room and I got sidetracked and I was playing with rocket. I pluged it in and pressed the button. It did nothing. I did it again. It shot fire everywhere and in a split second I dashed out of the room, so quick I looked like I was faster than lightning. The smock detectors went off for about an hour. My dad and I sat down on the back porch and we talked for about 5-10 minutes, and after the 10 minutes my dad got the truth out of me. I told him, "I know I did

(continued)

Model Responses to Writing Prompts

something stupid." After that my mom came and asked me what was wrong I told her the same thing I told my dad.

    Both of my parents told me what could of happened to me and the house and my dad, my brother, and mom. That day I really learned something important.

Score 5

This piece is mostly focused on the prompt. There is a chronological organizational pattern, as well as adequate development of events as the writer describes how he/she learned a lesson from "_____" about being responsible. Errors in sentence structure, punctuation, and spelling do not distract the reader.

One time my mom said to go shut the door that way the dog doesn't go outside and runaway or go in the nabors yard. I was to busies watching T.V. and I didn't go shut the door and my dog Jo Jo just ran right out of the house when I came back up stairs I ascked my mom where the dog was and she said did you shut the door and I said well... I gess I sort of forgot to shut the door. My mom just kept stairing at me. you what I said I forgot to shut the door. So me and my mom went outside and we started yelling Jo, Jo come back. You want a treat But he didn't come back so my nabor ____ came over and she said I saw your dog he's running over to the meaneys house. And I said will you help me get him and ____ said OK I'll help you get him and ____ and me ran to the meaneys yard and we caught Jo, and I picked him up and I started to hug him. Then right there I just rembered something that ____ she was being responcible she was

(continued)

Model Responses

helping me. Now I was going to help her and tnat why I learnd something inporant to. And that was to do something instead of Being lazzy. It was inportant to be responcible and It was inportant to me because ___ helped me when I needed the heep that was what was inportant. That was the end of the day for me ___, and JoJo.

Score 4

The response is focused on the topic and includes supporting details, yet lapses are present. This response could be more organized.

What I learned that is important is when I learned how to ride my bike.

I learned how to ride my bike in kindergarden. I learned with training wheels and then when I thought that I was was ready. My grandad took them off for me. I had peadled and peadled then off I went but I fell off. I did'nt have enough balanace to stay on. I tryed again and again till I got it right. I did'nt get it for two days. It was alot of falling, scrapes, and marks. I finally got it and I was so happy after wanting to give up but I did'nt give up instead I tryed till I had to go inside. I was proud, my mom, grandma, grandad, and dad. I stuffed away my training wheels just in case I need them. I went aroud the block with my mom on my bicycle without my training wheels. Now I know how to ride my bike without falling off and hurting myself like I dd in kindergarden.

Score 3

The writing is generally organized and focused on the topic of the importance of learning mathematics, although lapses occur. While the topic is developed, the writing includes irrelevant details. Sentence structure shows some variation. Knowledge of conventions and spelling is demonstrated.

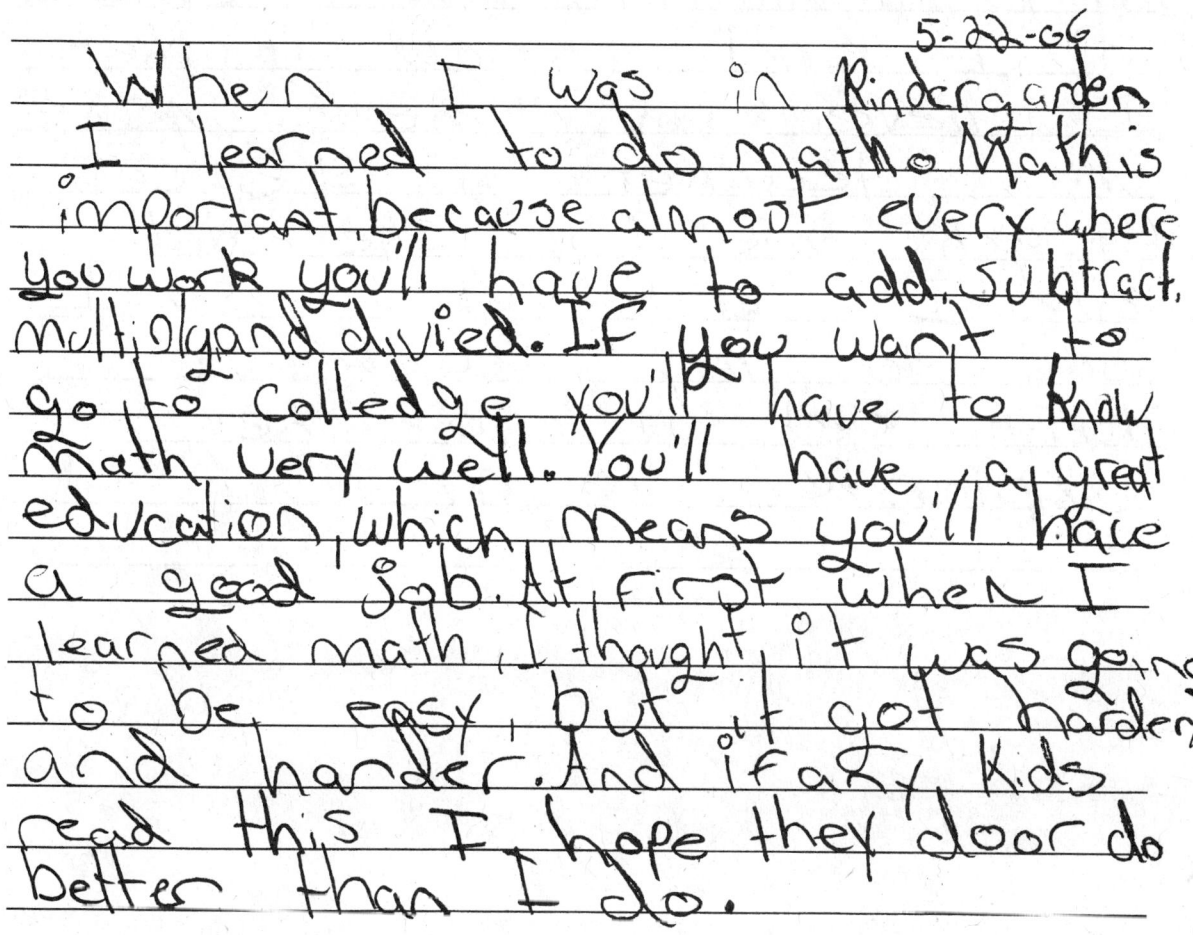

5-22-06

When I was in Kindergarden I learned to do math. Math is important because almost every where you work you'll have to add, subtract, multiply and divied. IF you want to go to colledge you'll have to know math very well. You'll have a great education, which means you'll have a good job. At first when I learned math, I thought it was going to be easy, but it got harder, and harder. And if any kids read this I hope they door do better than I do.

Model Responses

Score 2

This response shows a modest connection to the prompt. The writer explains how he/she learned to tell time. Awkward sentence construction, incomplete thoughts, and lack of punctuation are present.

Time is important to me because if I don't know it then I never now time I Asked my teacher if she can teach me so she did and I didn't get it so I said to my teacher I don't get it so she explaned to me

Model Responses

Score 1

This writing barely addresses the demands of the prompt. The writer tells about something he or she has learned, but fails to tell a story about how he or she learned it.

I hate 3, 4, and 12s. There so boring. I love to multiply. I like to beat everyone. It is fun!

I have to try doing 12s. If

Theme 2 Writing Prompt

In "The Family Tree," many of the animals were afraid that their family tree would be cut down.

Think about how they must have felt when the tree was not cut down.

Now write to explain how the animals felt once they knew that the tree would not be cut down.

Score 6

This writing sample represents a successful response to the prompt and shows a more sophisticated and personal understanding of the selection. In this response, the author uses his/her own experience and/or judgment to predict how the animals may have felt. With a few exceptions, punctuation, capitalization and spelling are correct. Various sentence structures are used.

> They might have been relieved and happy because they have been living there for a long time. The squirrels had stored all the nuts beneath the tree's roots. The woodpeckers got their food from the tree, and it had been going on for genarations. The female crow had its nest and her baby chicks. All these animals that had been living on the tree might have been very joyful because they could live on their nice, old home. They also might have been surprised to see that the tree was the woodcutter's Family Tree and that the woodcutters chose not to cut it down. The squirrels, the woodpeckers, and the crow were joyful, happy, and relieved that they could live there forever for genarations, and that they will have their tree, their home, back.

(continued)

Model Responses

They might have been thankful for the woodcutter who had said not to cut down the tree since it was his Family Tree because he could have said to cut down his Family Tree. The animals might have been feeling very good that their home wasn't going to be cut down with their family and their food. I think their most strongest and the most powerful feeling was being joyful and happy that the tree wasn't going to be cut down by the woodcutters.

Score 5

This short but focused response demonstrates that the author understood the selection and the task in the prompt. The response is appropriately organized and provides support based on the selection and the writer's prior knowledge. Word choice is appropriate and sentence structure is varied.

In the story The Family Tree a tree is going to be cut down. The crow worries that if the woodcutters are going to cut down the tree than her babies will come down with it. The squirral family worries that if they cut down the tree all the nuts will get lost. The woodcutters were painting red crosses on trees. He came to the family tree. He looked at the tree and saw inishals on it. It was his ma's and pa's inishals. He said, "We are not cutting down this tree." All the animals were happy.

Score 4

The response shows that the writer understood the story and responded to the task in the prompt. The response is appropriately organized giving the animals' feelings at the beginning of the selection (scared), continuing with relevant information from the selection, and ending with the animals' feelings at the end (happy). Word choice is appropriate and sentence structure is varied.

At the beging of the storie all the animals were scared because they thought that the wood cutters were gona cut their family tree down. The sound of them cutting other trees down got closer, and closer, and closer until they came to the animals family tree. Then one of the cutters relliesed that tree had his moms, and dads name on it. So they disidid to leve the tree standing. Then all the animals were happy.

Score 3

In this short response, the writer demonstrates understanding of the selection and addresses the task in the prompt. The supporting ideas are not developed with specific details from the selection. The response lacks a sense of completeness. Commonly used words are spelled correctly.

In this story "The Family Tree" I think at the end the animals felt happy. The tree the animals lived in for so long did not have to be cut down. So I know at the end the animals felt happy because they heard the man that was about to cut the tree down say he was not going to cut it down. The reason the man did not cut it down was because his mom and dad wrote thier name on it and he declared it the family tree. Those are some ways I know the animals felt happy at the end.

Score 2

The response does not represent a complete understanding of the selection, nor does it complete the task in the prompt. There is good use of information from the story, but the response does not answer the prompt. The response states that the animals were scared at the beginning of the story, but does not tell about their feelings when the tree is spared. The response lacks a sense of completeness.

In the story the animals were very scared that there were woodcuters cutting down the trees. There are families in the tree. The owl came by and warned them about the woodcuters. Then the mother crow dove down trying to keep the woodcuters away. The woodcuters got closer and closer. The tree was beautiful and old. It's been there for years now. The woodpeckers had a lot of time to peck bugs. The squirrel stored alot of nuts in the tree roots. The mother crow had babies in the nest.

Model Responses

Score 1

This writing sample minimally addresses the prompt. The response refers to events from the story but does not address the feelings of the animals when their tree was spared.

Once there was a family tree that was going to be cut down. When the owl saw the woodcutters he tould the other animals. All the animals must of been really sceard when they herd the news. The crows thaut that they had to pick out all the insects frum the tree. When the woodcutters saw the tree they desidid to not cut it down.

Model Responses

Theme 3 Writing Prompt

Suppose you had a pen pal who lived in another country.

Think about what you would tell your pen pal about your life.

Now write a letter telling your pen pal about your life.

Score 6

This response is well organized and cleverly written to meet the prompt in a cohesive and engaging way ("I heard that you were looking for a pen pal. So, I was wondering if you would be my pen pal as I to was looking for one in a different country too."). The well-selected details add to the writing and are accurately placed for smooth transitions.

Dear _____,

I heard that you were looking for a pen pal. So, I was wondering if you would be my pen pal as I to was looking for one in a different county too I also thought it would be conveinent if I started about myself now. If you want to be my pen pal these are some things you need to know, such as my hobbies and all that stuff.

This is how I start my day. "Honey wake up!" I hear in my ear as I feel the sheets brush off my body and onto the floor. Yep! You guessed it, it's my mom trying to get me out of the bed after

(continued)

Model Responses

a long day I had yesturday
I quikly got dressed then, redize
I have a big test. So I try all
the monuvers to get of school,
but my mom can see right though
me. So I have to go to school.
After shool is over I go home then
have a snack. After I eat I go
to dance class, for TWO hours. Then,
I come home and do my night routine.
    I have visited France once and in
don't know very much about your living
conditions, but I do know that some
people over there are very friendly
So, I would like to hear your
daily sceadule too. Please write
back telling if you want to be
my pen pal soon.

            From,

Score 5

This is a focused and organized response. The opening is quite creative, explaining that she has not written to her pen pal on the computer because it broke so she has decided to write a letter. There are effective transitions that keep the story moving along and cohesive. Some details are less important and may be seen as extraneous. This keeps this response from a 6.

Dear Pen Pal I'm sorry that I haven't been able to talk to you in the computer. The reason is that my computer broke down so I decited to write you a letter. Me and my sisster been dieying to tell you what we did over this Summer. First we went to New York to visit ant ___ for a week then we came back to Florida. Second we went to Disney World for two weeks. We stayed in the most beautaful hotel I have ever seen. The next day we went to the magic Kindom. We took pictues with Cindrela, Bell, Jasmin, Minny and Mickie mouse. After that we went to many rides. The last day I went to MGM studios. We went to the hunted monssion when we came out we were so scared that we couldn't even walk. Then at night at am 2:00 we were realy sleepy

(continued)

Model Responses

that night. When we got back to Florida we went to sleep right away. Then the last week of summer vacation we went to the beach. We stayed ther for one whole day. The next day I went to my friends house to spent the night her name is _____ we been friends since 2nd grade. She is realy funny you should talk to her she is friendly. One Sunday night I went to bed at 9:00 p.m. On Monday I was early to school. I had a great 1st day of school. I hope you write me back. Bye!!.!.!.

love,
_____

Score 4

This letter is organized and focused. Details are many but presented in a simple list style, limiting the depth of information. Sentences are simple, well spelled, and appropriately punctuated. While some of the ideas are followed up with additional information, that information is in the format of lists ("The wars I read about are the revolutionary wars, Civil war, and the russian and the french war.").

Dear, pen pal

This is my life. I like sports, war, and history. The sports I like are football, basketball, and baseball. The wars I read about are th revalutionary wars, civil war, and the russian and the french war. I also like watching sports and these are my favorite teams. bears, cubs, bulls, illini, pistons, whitesox, steelers, colts, chargers, 49ers, seahawks, giants, blackhawks, mallards, bengals, falcons, and the panthers. I also like to liston to music. My favorite bands are nickelback, green day, and crossfade. My moms and dads names are _____, and _____. My sisters name is _____. My pets names are _____, and _____. At recess I play football, basketball, and berglers.

Model Responses

Score 3

This response exhibits an attempt at organization with details supporting ideas. The student seems to be writing more about America than about her own personal experience. She does however explain her opinion of American food, music and clothing. Solid comprehension is lessened by weak sentence structure and grammatical errors.

We have a Lot of veriaty in our food. I Lisin to all kinds of music like Rock, County. Our outfits are mostly a T-shirt and jeans.

Our food is Chinec food witch is like garlic chicken. Their is Mexic food too like tacos. Amrican food like pizza and hamburger.

Our music is like Rock witch I lisin to a Lot. Then their is County witch I lisin to also lisin to but not as much. Last but not least Rap witch I hate.

Our outfits are like comefutabal T-shirts. In the summer is shorts. In the winter or spring it is jeans.

Model Responses

T58

© Harcourt • Grade 3

Score 2

The pen pal letter does include some relevant information but there is no organization. Limited vocabulary and sparse supporting details, along with errors in grammar and punctuation, all affect readability. Most of the details merely mention that either Philadelphia or school is fun without explaining what specifically about these places is fun.

I would like to tall about phadelphia I go to _____ school. and I love philadelphia. I would love to met your wold. it's fun in philadelphia because we go to ris in phladelphia have fun we Do fun work in _____ school. and have fun. We read Book in _____ school. and stut hrod and work hrd. We Do Fwor home work every Day.

Score 1

This response is a list of items that the writer could use in a pen pal letter. The student does not actually write a letter. Knowledge of sentence structure is not evidenced since writing is very brief.

I would tell him/or her that my name is ___ and were I live my favrote color fovorte food and sport weve I am from

Theme 4 Writing Prompt

When we use our imagination, we can go anywhere.

Think about taking a trip to another planet.

Now write a story about taking a trip to another planet.

Score 6

This engaging story is well developed with a clear, chronological beginning, middle, and end. The sentences are maturely crafted with a variety of structures, clever dialogue, and precise word choice. The writer successfully uses a variety of language conventions.

There once was a girl named Lilly. Lilly had always dreamed of visiting Mercury and Pluto.

One day on Lilly's 23 birthday her mom said "For your birthday Lilly, your father and I got you a very special gift. We signed you up to be an astronot!" Lilly was thrilled. "Oh thank you mom. Thank you dad!" Lilly said as she hipped and hopped with joy.

Lilly practiced going up in space every day until the day had come. Her captin had said "Lilly you have done a wonderful job here. You have proved that you are ready!" Lilly was thrilled yet again. So she climbed on bord the Space Travel 2000. "Start count down!"

(continued)

Model Responses

one of the controlers said. "5,4,3,2,1, BLAST OFF!" Lilly said. "Off to Mercury!" Lilly finally got to mercury. Lilly was swetting in a split second! "This place is too hot!" Lilly complained. "5,4,3,2,1, BLAST OFF!" Lilly yelled. "Off to Pluto!" Lilly finally loned on Pluto. "Burrr. Too C-c-cold!" Lilly complained. Lilly's helmet had iceicls hanging. "5,4,3,2,1, BLAST OFF!" Lilly said sadly.

When Lilly got back she said "Earth is the place to be. Not too hot, not too cold." Lilly was happy to be back were she belongs, Earth.

Score 5

This response addresses the prompt quite successfully with sequentially organized story events supported by interesting details. The writer's emotional response to events ("My heart was pumping as a chill went through my spine.") gives the text a strong voice. There are occasional spelling errors and lapses in punctuation, but they do not impede communication.

It has been my deam to be an astrnot and fly to space and it is finaly coming true! It started at the count down 5, 4, 3, My heart was pumping as a chill went through my spine then 2, 1 Blastof! we were shooting up in the rocket it felt like a miricle. I was nervose but I was sure nothing would go wrong but I was to exited to think about any thing else then the moon and if Something could be living there. The Rocket seemed to be a smoother ride when we got higher. I looked out the window a saw stars there were millons of them it was unbelievable! The next moment we had stoped I knew that we had landed the rocket. It was my turn to go out I put my space suit on, took a deep breath and took one big step on the moon I bonced of of it like a trampaline I was having a great time when, I listened I herd strang noises I new that I was the only astronot on the moon so who could it be I crept behind a big rock and saw

(continued)

Model Responses

2 green little men. I was shocked this was the first human life ever in history of the world we left them alone because we needed to know more about them first, but that was not my job I'll come to the moon some other time and find out but now it was time to go back to earth. we blasted of and the next second we were safe on ground. We only told the space craft about the strang 2 green little men. that's another story to find out I hope to some day go back to space a see those 2 little green men.

Score 4

This response is a generally organized story with some details about a trip to Venus. Some sections are confusing, repetitive, or extraneous to the development of the piece. Word choice and use of conventions are adequate, and there is an attempt to vary sentence structure and length.

A Trip To Venus!

Oh yeah! Oh yeah! I Finally started my journey to Venus. Could you believe that Roxanna. We are actually going through outer space.

When we got a little bit farther away from Earth we saw Venus. I asked Roxanna to land the space craft there. I thought it was really pretty and so did Roxanna.

Finally, we landed I said five minutes later. Roxanna had finally made the plane to land, and I was already outside. I was hopping around almost everything there was. But there wasn't much. Even though, I felt very joyful.

Sometimes, Roxanna said I was acting weird. But anyways, I didn't believe her. I was so happy that I was havieng a conversation to myself. Not even I knew what had gotten into me.

Then Roxanna anounced to me that we had to be heading back. I didn't want to leave. So Roxanna had to pull me into the spacecraft.

(continued)

Model Responses

Then we got a little bit farther away from Venus and I could see the Earth. I was excited for seeing the Earth My home planet. Even though at the same time I was sad for leaving Venus. Then I thought that I could come back again. so I didn't feel that bad.

Score 3

This response focuses on the prompt, and there is an attempt at organization, yet there is no real ending. In his/her description of "moving to Pluto," the writer demonstrates some knowledge of what life in space might be like. Lack of punctuation and capitalization somewhat compromises meaning.

once I was going to move and we move to a planet name pluto it was very small I't didn't have no houses and no food we couldn't survive and we didn't have spaceshoes are helment are suite it was so hot we didn't have nothing to were itself the close that we been wearing for two days we didnt no water are nothing we couldn't survive without Auxugine And that my storie abou bein on a planet.

Score 2

The writing is related to the prompt. It has a beginning and end and includes some details that support the story's main idea, yet thoughts are presented in random fashion. Errors in sentence construction and punctuation slightly affect comprehension.

Once a ponna time, A kid name Joe wanted to travel to Jupiter, Mars, Uranus Joe was only 9 years old. He want NASA for a space ship. His first planet was Uranas. Joe was a bravest kid Joe really liked in space he is sometimes in scared. He sometimes brings friends with him. When he finish with his missions he was glad he was back. The End

Score 1

This brief response addresses the topic of a trip to another planet, yet meaning is nearly impossible to construct due to numerous errors in spelling and punctuation.

I would go to plodo in my imagination. So I mate find now anumols and new people I mit find a now plas to live in. Plodo is a bifrint plant nobote is aver ben on are sen ina eye.

Model Responses

Theme 5 Writing Prompt

Most people have been part of a team.

Think about a time when you were part of a team.

Now explain what you did to help the team.

Score 6

This story is well-crafted and organized very logically – preparation for going to the race, helping everyone get ready just prior to the race, helping a younger racer, finishing the race, and feelings about helping a teammate. Effective use of dialogue and transitions make the text interesting. Slight confusion in verb tense does not interfere with comprehension.

I am apart of _____ sailing racing team. Today we are going to a race in Clearwater. It is suppose to be very windy. So we pack jackets we brought extras for other teammates. It might be useful to bring snacks to. After all you do get pretty hungry. We were on our way! When we got there we helped everyone get their boats down from the trailer. All of us had to rig our boats. Everybody helps the little kids. Next it was time for the race to begin. We shouted our sail numbers to the boat who was marking the scores. Yes time to begin. Uh oh! As we left A kid's sail tie broke. I noticed he didn't have any extras. I was going towards him and he yelled" can you help me?" After hearing that I sailed as fast as I could when I got

(continued)

Model Responses

over there I could see he was only seven years old and was crying. "I said it will be all right look I have an extra." He stopped crying as after he heard that. When I fixed his sail all up he thanked me and sailed away. It felt good helping one of my teammates. Finally when we finished the race we were all glad and started sailing to shore. We put are boats away and as I was about to leave I said to the seven year old boy "good job". As you can see helping teammates is a good thing to do.

Score 5

This response is focused on the topic helping a team. Ideas that are supported by details and examples, and well-placed transitions make the paper easy to read. Writing conventions, word choice, and sentence construction all contribute to this well-written response. Some more specific examples would have earned this response a score of 6.

I've been part of a team called "Odessey of the Mind". I did quite a lot to help my team, but let's not include my bossiness.

One thing I did for my team was I brought in a yellow shirt, two inches of construction paper and some cardboard. My team and I used a lot of the construction paper. That yellow shirt got used too it wa used for the panther. Now, the card board was used for a big tree on the edge of the scene.

Another thing I did for the team was memorize my lines. It was hard to memorize my lines but I did it in two weeks. Even though I didn't like my lines, I had no choice to like them or not.

I also helped my team by helping paint the scenery. It took a long time to get the scenery done, but we got it done in time with a lot of help from me and my team.

My team and I got our project

(continued)

Model Responses

done just in time I could not have done it without them and I bet they could not have done it without me either, becaus one person does not make a team.

The End

Score 4

This football story indirectly addresses the prompt. No mention is made of *helping* a team, but the writer relates how he scored a winning touchdown. Confusion of verb tense and lack of supporting details and examples somewhat affect understanding. Errors in sentence structure, punctuation, and capitalization are also present in this response.

Me and my Football team

Hello My name is _____ And soon I got Go to my football pratice. But I really dont want to go. But my dad Knows I'm scared to play but he signed me up any way! So I had to go to the pratice. And when I got there guess what my coach wanted me to be the running back. And I said okay I'll be the runningback. So he set up play and said blue 49 blue 49 and the coach told me okay kid your getting the ball. I said Im getting the what. And I said well coach I dont know how to play football. Well can you at least do one play. well okay the coach Said the play again blue 49 blue 49 and I got the ball and I ran it all the way to the tochdown. and then a few days later in the game it was 10 seconds left in the they therw the ball and I score

Score 3

The writer begins with a strong emphasis on the prompt, but difficulty maintaining focus on the main idea weakens the response ("... and I will keep playing tennis until I get better than my dad."). Organization of ideas is not always evident and some details are extraneous.

One day I helped my tennis team by winning king and queen of the courts. It was a realy hard battle that day. But I helped my team because we were loosing. But the worst thing was that we were playing against 7th graders and the good thing was we won. But befor I can tell that part I have to finish my whole storie. Okay, now lets get back to my storie. We were out there for an hour it was a hard hour that was a big battle. Iv been playing tennis for 3 years and next year it will be my 4th year playing tennis and I will keep playing tennis until I get better than my dad. Then I will play baseball but now I'll get back to the storie okay now. well I was beeting the 7th graders and I had some help from my team to then we finally won. We got real meatals they had a tennis ball on them and a tennis racket and a tennis count.

Score 2

This response focuses on playing on a team. However, lack of details and organization keep this a low 2.

I Play ball in the park I Play to have fun, I like the boys on my team. I help the team win We Shake hands after the game. Cheer for good play, We lern to be good sports,

Score 1

This response addresses the prompt, although organization is weak and irrelevant information is included. Errors in spelling and grammar throughout interfere with understanding.

I help my team for we culd get ponts and get candy. My table team it name is ____ if we get olot of ponts like 99 we get to go to coputer of get pencil. At Pe we whet and we neddet to play baiss ball and I ditjed play and it was my fallt my team lost and all was so sad and I said sorry I did't play and they said that ok ____ and I said will you forget me and they set yes and I said do you what to play and they say lets go and we whent we whet so happy we when to the class we woked hard and we win. we got 99 ponts we whent to coputer and we played alot of games.

Model Responses

Theme 6 Writing Prompt

The Arctic Circle is an interesting region to explore.

Think about what you learned about the Arctic.

Now write a report about what you learned about the Arctic.

Score 6

This writing sample represents a good summary report of the information from the four selections. The organization is well-crafted. The short introduction and conclusion represent an attempt to hold the report together and make it interesting. The writer uses his/her own words in reporting information from the selections ("Early in the 1900's it was like a race to get to the North Pole."). Various sentence structures are used.

From reading about the Arctic Circl I think it would be an interesting place to explore. But it would be cold. I learned that the Arctic Circle is the area around the North Pole. It has islands, an ocaen and parts of some countries like Canada, Denmark, Norway Sweden Finland Russia, Iceland and America. The largest island is Greenland. Its warmer in th summer in the Artic Circle, and th sun hardley sets There is a day in the winter when the sun never shines.

I learned that lots of people wanted to explore the Arctic Circle and make it to the Northpole. Early in the 1900's it was like a

(continued)

Model Responses

race to get to the North pole. but Robert Pery and Mathew Henson may have been the first to get there. They had a hard trip in 1989 and took lots of people with them.

I liked the part about the animals and the plants the best. I learned that the polar bears are one of the largest bears on Earth and they have hair on the bottoms of there feet to keep them from falling on the ice. There are also arctic foxes the size of cats there. Their fur color changes. There are also plants and flowers there like saxifrage, mountain avens and Iceland arctic poppy.

The Arctic Circk would be an interesting place to go.

Score 5

This response answers the prompt showing understanding of what has been read. The writer attempts to include as much information as possible from the four selections. The organizational pattern is evident; the writer moves from one of the selections to another in order, stating and summarizing as much information as possible. Word choice is appropriate, and sentence structure is varied.

The Arctic would be a interesting place to go to but it would be very cold. The Arctic is very cold but we can still learn about it. Robert Peary and Matthew Henson said they were they frist ones to reach the Arctic but Another man Frederick Cook said he reched the Arctic first but scientists think Peary and Henson were the first to rech the Arctic. Today the scienests think that not Cook or Peary and Henson rech the Arctic circle. The polar bears are one of largest bear on earth. The have think oily white fur. Their fur porects them when they are swining in icy waters. On land their lage feet act like snowshoes. The hair on the bottom of the polar bears feet help them walk without slipping on the ice. Arctic foxes are they size as a cat but not a pet! They have short legs and short ears and a long bushy tail. In summer their fur truns to a grayish brown. In the winter their fur turns white so it is hard to see him. Like polar bears foxes have hair to not slip on the ice. Saxfrage is a plant that can grow in between rocks. It means rock-breaker. Mountains avens is also a flowering plant. It is a part of the rose family. The are yellow and white. The arctic Iceland

(continued)

Model Responses

poppy has white, orange or red flowers. The flower lasts a long time. The have a strong scent Some times the sun never comes up in a day! They have research site at the Arctic circle. The North pole is the center of land and water found inside the Arctic circle. The Arctic the area just outside the North pole. It is made up of islands The Arctic and northern area are made up be several countries. In the summertime it is warmer there. This is the Arctic Circle

Score 4

The writing sample is generally focused on the topic and shows understanding of what has been read. The writing is organized as a report presenting the information that is important to the writer. The writer attempts to interest readers with an introduction ("The North Pole is cool.") and conclusion ("The North Pole is fun to learn about."). Word choice is appropriate, and sentence structure is varied.

The North Pole is cool. Robert Peary and Matthew Henson were the first ones to go to the North Pole. Frederick Cook thought he was the first one to the North Pole but the first ones to the North Pole was Peary and Henson. Polar Bears are the largest bear on Earth. The hair on the bottom of Polar Bear's feet helps them walk without slipping. Arctic foxe's fur turns grayish brown in the summer. Saxifrage has about 300 species of it. Mountain avens are part of the rose family. Arctic Iceland Poppy's white, orange, and red flowers have a strong sent. In the summer, the sun hardly sets. In the North Pole the night lasts longer. The largest island is almost completely inside the Arctic circle. The North Pole is fun to learn about.

Model Responses

Score 3

This response represents partial success in writing a report about what has been learned. The writing is generally on topic, but the writer focuses on what is interesting to him/her instead of all of the information from the selections. Word choice is appropriate, and sentence structure is simple.

I've learn a lot about the Arctic. One thing I learned was that the North Pole isn't even on land and is the center of the Arctic circle. I also learned that the sun hardly sets in the summer and hardly rises in the winter. One thing I thought was interesting was that there are flower in the arctic. It was great learning about the arctic.

Score 2

This response represents a weak attempt to write a report. Writing is related to the topic but only refers to one selection: "Explore the Arctic." Word choice is limited and sentence structure is simple.

I lerned that polar bears have fur on there feed so they won't slep on ice. I lerned that Arctic foxes are as big as a cat. Arctic foxes have short legs to. Arctic foxes also have short ears They have a bushy tail. Sax is a plant. It can grow between rocks. It's name means rock-breaker. The flowers can be different colors. Mountain avens is also a flowering plant. It is a part of the rose family. The plant generally have yellow or white flowers.

Model Responses

Score 1

This brief response represents an attempt to answer the prompt, but the response is minimal showing lack of understanding of the task in the prompt. There is no evidence of an organizational pattern; any supporting ideas are presented in a disorganized list. Sentence structure is simple, although punctuation and spelling are correct. The writer used "investigated" (spelled correctly – another form of the word is used in the selection) for "explored" in referring to Peary and Henson.

The first people are peary and henson. They were there in 1909. They investigated the arctic circle. The Arctic fox is about the same size as a cat. The poler bear is the biggest bear in the world. The sun hardly sets. The noth pole is the senter of all the land and water foun inside the arctic circle. Greenland is the largest island. It o most completey is inside the antic curcle.

Model Responses

Twists and Turns — Theme 1

Name _____ Date _____

Performance Summary

	Student Score
READING	
Reading Comprehension	
Multiple-Choice Items	_____/18
Short-Response Open-Ended Item	_____/2
Extended-Response Open-Ended Item	_____/4
Phonics/Spelling	_____/15
Robust Vocabulary	_____/10
Total Student Reading Score	_____/49
LANGUAGE ARTS	
Grammar	_____/10
WRITING	_____/6
ORAL READING FLUENCY	
Passage 1	_____ Words Correct Per Minute
Passage 2	_____ Words Correct Per Minute

(Bubble in the appropriate performance level.)

Reading

Below Basic	Basic (On-Level)	Proficient (On-Level)	Advanced
1–20	21–30	31–40	41–49
○	○	○	○

Language Arts

Below Basic	Basic (On-Level)	Proficient (On-Level)	Advanced
1–4	5–6	7–8	9–10
○	○	○	○

Writing

Below Basic	Basic (On-Level)	Proficient (On-Level)	Advanced
1–2	3–4	5	6
○	○	○	○

Oral Reading Fluency

25th Percentile	50th Percentile	75th Percentile	90th Percentile
44 WCPM	71 WCPM	99 WCPM	128 WCPM
○	○	○	○

Grateful acknowledgment is made to Highlights for Children, Inc., Columbus, Ohio, for permission to reprint "An Earful" by Dale-Marie Bryan, illustrated by Erin Mauterer from *Highlights for Children* Magazine, January 2005. Copyright © 2005 by Highlights for Children, Inc.

Copyright © by Harcourt, Inc.

All rights reserved. No part of this publication may be reproduced or transmitted in any form or by any means, electronic or mechanical, including photocopy, recording, or any information storage and retrieval system, without permission in writing from the publisher.

Permission is hereby granted to individuals using the corresponding student's textbook or kit as the major vehicle for regular classroom instruction to photocopy entire pages from this publication in classroom quantities for instructional use and not for resale. Requests for information on other matters regarding duplication of this work should be addressed to School Permissions and Copyrights, Harcourt, Inc., 6277 Sea Harbor Drive, Orlando, Florida 32887-6777. Fax: 407-345-2418.

HARCOURT and the Harcourt Logo are trademarks of Harcourt, Inc., registered in the United States of America and/or other jurisdictions.

Printed in the United States of America

ISBN 10 0-15-368492-5
ISBN 13 978-0-15-368492-0 (Package of 12)

9 10   1409   16 15 14 13 12 11 10

If you have received these materials as examination copies free of charge, Harcourt School Publishers retains title to the materials and they may not be resold. Resale of examination copies is strictly prohibited and is illegal.

Possession of this publication in print format does not entitle users to convert this publication, or any portion of it, into electronic format.

Name _____

Theme Test
Theme 1

Reading Comprehension

▶ Read the article "Pine Cone Critter" before answering Numbers 1 through 6.

Pine Cone Critter

Pine cones are great for many things. Brightly painted pine cones make beautiful decorations. A pine cone can also be made into an animal, or critter. But you won't find this critter crawling around in the forest. You can take your critter anywhere you want.

You and your friends can make a whole critter community. Pretend the critters are learning in school, going out to play, or exploring in the forest.

What You Need:
- one pine cone
- two plastic craft eyes
- a small piece of brown or black felt (4 inches tall and 4 inches wide)
- one small pompom
- colored markers
- safety scissors
- glue

How to Make the Critter:
1) Cut the felt into four equal pieces (about 1 inch tall and 1 inch wide each).
2) Cut two paw shapes out of two pieces of felt.
3) Glue the felt paws to the bottom of the pine cone.
4) Cut two ear shapes out of the other two pieces of felt.
5) Glue the felt ears to the pine cone.

Reading Comprehension

GO ON

Name _____

6) Glue the plastic craft eyes near the top of the pine cone.

7) Glue the pompom to the back of the pine cone to make a tail.

8) Use the markers to color a mouth and nose on the pine cone.

Now give your pine cone a name. You and your friends can imagine what your pine cone critters will do. Will they live in a forest? Will they walk to school together? Where will they play? Enjoy your pine-cone community of friends!

Name _____

Theme Test
Theme 1

▶ **Now answer Numbers 1 through 6. Base your answers on the article "Pine Cone Critter."**

1. What is the title of this article?
   - Ⓐ "What You Will Need"
   - Ⓑ "How to Make the Critter"
   - Ⓒ "Pine Cone Critter"
   - Ⓓ "Pine Cones are Great for Many Things"

2. Where in your science book would you look to find more information about pine cones?
   - Ⓕ index
   - Ⓖ title page
   - Ⓗ front cover
   - Ⓘ review questions

3. Which word comes FIRST in alphabetical order?
   - Ⓐ pine
   - Ⓑ cone
   - Ⓒ critter
   - Ⓓ community

4. Which of these will you need to make a pine cone critter?
   - Ⓕ fur
   - Ⓖ glue
   - Ⓗ paint
   - Ⓘ crayons

Reading Comprehension

GO ON

Name _____

Theme Test

Theme 1

5. Which of the following might you find in a dictionary?
   - Ⓐ a picture of a pine cone
   - Ⓑ places to get pompoms
   - Ⓒ a story about forest animals
   - Ⓓ directions for making a pine cone critter

6. When making a pine cone critter, what happens to the piece of felt?
   - Ⓕ The felt changes the pine cone's color.
   - Ⓖ The felt is cut into a tail.
   - Ⓗ The felt covers the pine cone critter.
   - Ⓘ The felt is made into ears and paws.

Reading Comprehension

GO ON

Name _____

Theme Test
Theme 1

▶ Read the story "Sam's Morning" before answering Numbers 7 through 13.

Sam's Morning

This Monday morning at Sam's house was very similar to other Monday mornings. The weekend had been relaxing and pleasurable, but Monday morning always felt rushed as Sam got ready for school and his parents got ready for work. Everyone in the family scampered around the house and bumped into each other. To make matters even worse, it was raining.

After Sam finished breakfast, he went to his desk to organize the papers and books he would need for school. However, to Sam's surprise, his desk was bare. He was shocked and could feel his stomach churning because he knew the bus would arrive soon. Sam quickly checked the floor and his top left desk drawer, but there was just not enough time to search thoroughly. Sam sometimes had trouble keeping track of his school supplies, but he had never misplaced all of his materials.

Sam asked his parents if they had seen his homework papers. Sam's father said it was too late to look for them anymore, because if Sam waited any longer he might miss the bus. His mother shook her head and smiled. Sam had worked hard all weekend on a research report about the Grand Canyon. He just could not bear the thought that he had lost his report. It was due to his teacher first thing in the morning. Sam's stomach began to tighten even more.

Sam was very frustrated. He picked up his backpack as if to throw it. He was surprised to feel how heavy it was. When Sam opened the backpack, he discovered that it was full of all the papers and books he thought he was missing! Sam had placed

Reading Comprehension

GO ON

them in his backpack on Sunday afternoon, after he had finished his homework. Sam was relieved.

　He laughed because he forgot that he had remembered to prepare. He darted out the door to catch the bus, which was creeping up to his house. His mother watched him through the window. She just shook her head and smiled.

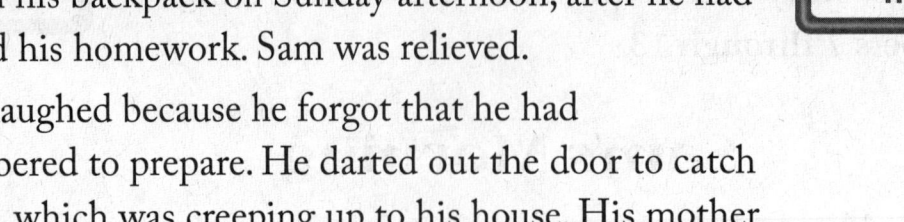

Name _____

Theme Test
Theme 1

▶ **Now answer Numbers 7 through 13. Base your answers on the story "Sam's Morning."**

7. Where does this story MOSTLY take place?
   Ⓐ at school
   Ⓑ on the bus
   Ⓒ at Sam's house
   Ⓓ outside in the rain

8. Why did the author include the picture of Sam?
   Ⓕ to show the ending of the story
   Ⓖ to show that Sam worked very hard
   Ⓗ to show readers why Sam's house is so busy
   Ⓘ to prove that Sam really did do his homework

9. What is the title of this story?
   Ⓐ "Monday"
   Ⓑ "In a Rush"
   Ⓒ "Where is it?"
   Ⓓ "Sam's Morning"

10. Which of the following would come FIRST in alphabetical order?
    Ⓕ book
    Ⓖ missing
    Ⓗ backpack
    Ⓘ homework

Reading Comprehension

GO ON

Name _____

Theme Test

Theme 1

11. Which word BEST describes Sam?

    Ⓐ lazy

    Ⓑ careful

    Ⓒ forgetful

    Ⓓ dishonest

12. Which word BEST describes Sam's mother?

    Ⓕ slow

    Ⓖ angry

    Ⓗ amused

    Ⓘ frustrated

13. Explain two things you learn about Sam and his family from the story. Use details and information from the story to support your answer.

    _____
    _____
    _____
    _____
    _____
    _____
    _____

Reading Comprehension

Name _____

**Theme Test
Theme 1**

▶ Read the story "An Earful" before answering Numbers 14 through 20.

An Earful
by Dale-Marie Bryan
illustrated by Erin Mauterer

"Your homework is to collect sounds," Mrs. Olson said. She handed out sheets of paper shaped like giant ears. Then she held up a shiny blue kazoo. "Everyone who gets an 'earful' will get one of these." The class laughed.

Later, Jacob glared out the school-bus window. Not fair, he thought. How could he collect enough sounds on his family's farm? There were plenty of noises in town. If only he lived where tires squealed and sirens wailed.

Jacob scrambled off the bus when it screeched to a stop at his mailbox. But he wasn't in the mood to wave as it drove away.

When he threw open the gate, it groaned. That was how he felt about his homework.

On the porch, Jacob knelt beside the kittens curled on the rug. They sounded like tiny motors when they purred.

"I'm home!" Jacob called. He thumped his book bag down on a kitchen chair.

The rocker in the nursery stopped creaking.

"How was school?" his mother asked walking in with his baby brother on her shoulder. She was patting his little back.

"I've got homework," Jacob grumbled.

Reading Comprehension

GO ON

Name _____

Theme Test
Theme 1

The baby burped, and Jacob laughed. "That's what I think about it, too!"

"Have a snack before you do your chores," his mother said. She took the animal crackers down from the cupboard.

Jacob rattled the carton. Not many left. He crunched two tigers, three lions, and a seal, then gulped down some milk. *Grrr, roar, ork!* If only animal crackers were real. He would have plenty of noises to list!

Goldie, Jacob's collie, woofed as Jacob walked toward the barn. Her puppies were yipping in a straw-filled stall. Jacob plinked dog-food pellets into their pan and the pups snuffled and crunched.

How could Jacob collect enough sounds on the farm?

In the chicken house, Jacob shooed two cackling hens from their nests. He slipped their warm eggs into his jacket. Wouldn't it be funny if he forgot about the eggs and they hatched? He'd have a peeping pocket!

In the corral, a black cow napped in the sun. Jacob woke her when he poured corn into her pan. "*Moo*, thank you!" she seemed to say.

Tap, clatter, clink. Dad drove the tractor into the yard. The lid on the tractor's smokestack rattled when it chuffed and chugged to a stop.

"How was school?" Dad asked, stepping down from the cab.

Reading Comprehension

GO ON

Name _____

Theme Test
Theme 1

Jacob shrugged. "OK, I guess," he said. "I have some homework."

Jacob put the eggs in the kitchen, then climbed to his tree house. He could see Dad's beehives by the hay field. Six hives usually meant plenty of humming. But today he couldn't hear it over the scolding of the blue jays and the chattering of the sparrows. How could a person think?

"QUIET!" Jacob shouted.

Suddenly, he sat up straight. Cows mooed and puppies yipped. Chickens cackled in their yard. When Goldie began barking below, Jacob grinned. There were plenty of noises on the farm. "I hear you!" he called. He hurried down from the tree. He had an earful of homework to do.

Name _____

Theme Test
Theme 1

▶ **Now answer Numbers 14 through 20. Base your answers on the story "An Earful."**

14. Where does the story MOSTLY take place?
    - Ⓐ in town
    - Ⓑ at school
    - Ⓒ on a farm
    - Ⓓ on a school bus

15. Who wrote this story?
    - Ⓕ Jacob Goldie
    - Ⓖ Erin Mauterer
    - Ⓗ Charlotte Smith
    - Ⓘ Dale-Marie Bryan

16. At the beginning of the story, how does Jacob feel about his homework assignment?
    - Ⓐ annoyed
    - Ⓑ bored
    - Ⓒ excited
    - Ⓓ happy

17. Where would you find the word kazoo in the dictionary?
    - Ⓕ After apple and before cup
    - Ⓖ After dandy and before flea
    - Ⓗ After jazz and before monkey
    - Ⓘ After centimeter and before honey

Reading Comprehension   GO ON

Name _____

Theme Test
Theme 1

18. How has Jacob changed at the end of the story?
    A He has learned to listen.
    B He wants to move to the city.
    C He no longer cares about his chores.
    D He takes better care of the animals on the farm.

19. Read the sentence from the story.

    "I've got homework," Jacob grumbled.

    Which word would come FIRST if you put them in alphabetical order?
    F got
    G I've
    H grumbled
    I homework

Name _____

Theme Test
Theme 1

20. How does Jacob's attitude toward his homework and his home change? Use details and information from the story to support your answer.

Reading Comprehension

14

STOP

© Harcourt • Grade 3

Name _____

Theme Test
Theme 1

Phonics/Spelling

▶ For Numbers 21 through 29, read each model word. Then fill in the circle next to the word that has the same vowel sound and completes each sentence.

21. c<u>a</u>t

   Don't leave home without your _____.

   Ⓐ hat
   Ⓑ gloves
   Ⓒ cape
   Ⓓ coat

22. m<u>o</u>p

   The farmer was worried about the _____.

   Ⓕ pig
   Ⓖ hen
   Ⓗ dog
   Ⓘ rooster

23. t<u>u</u>b

   I love to _____.

   Ⓐ run
   Ⓑ skip
   Ⓒ rut
   Ⓓ swim

Phonics/Spelling

GO ON

Name _____

Theme Test
Theme 1

24. fin

    Please give the book to _____.

    Ⓕ them
    Ⓖ him
    Ⓗ her
    Ⓘ dime

25. pen

    The paint was _____.

    Ⓐ sticky
    Ⓑ purple
    Ⓒ green
    Ⓓ wet

26. bait

    I had to hurry because Bob would not _____.

    Ⓕ box
    Ⓖ wait
    Ⓗ walk
    Ⓘ come

27. each

    I won't _____ any more paper.

    Ⓐ want
    Ⓑ need
    Ⓒ have
    Ⓓ peach

Phonics/Spelling

GO ON

Name _____

Theme Test
Theme 1

28. r<u>ai</u>n

    Please give the horse some _____.

    Ⓕ hay
    Ⓖ oats
    Ⓗ main
    Ⓘ apples

29. gr<u>oa</u>n

    I was hoping she would come with me to the _____.

    Ⓐ fair
    Ⓑ show
    Ⓒ play
    Ⓓ movie

Phonics/Spelling

GO ON

Name _____

Theme Test
Theme 1

▶ **Choose the best word to complete each sentence for Numbers 30 through 35.**

30. I like _____ them dance.
    - F watch
    - G watched
    - H watching
    - I watchful

31. I _____ on her door to see if she was home.
    - A knock
    - B knocked
    - C knocking
    - D knockless

32. It is wet because it has been _____ all day.
    - F rain
    - G rained
    - H raining
    - I rainful

33. The _____ were full of birds.
    - A bush
    - B bushs
    - C bushes
    - D bushess

Phonics/Spelling

18

GO ON

© Harcourt • Grade 3

Name _____

Theme Test
Theme 1

34. The boys slept in bunk _____.
   - F bed
   - G beds
   - H bedes
   - I bedds

35. It is hard to care for two _____ at once.
   - A baby
   - B babys
   - C babies
   - D babyes

Phonics/Spelling

Name _____

Robust Vocabulary

Theme Test
Theme 1

▶ **Choose the best word to complete each sentence for Numbers 36 through 45.**

36. While playing the game "follow the leader," Carlos _____ everything that Matt did.
    - (F) recited
    - (G) imitated
    - (H) murmured
    - (I) autographed

37. When Ling couldn't figure out the answer, she became very _____.
    - (A) donated
    - (B) pleasant
    - (C) concealed
    - (D) frustrated

38. Maria knows how to do many things; she is a _____ girl.
    - (F) loyal
    - (G) shabby
    - (H) talented
    - (I) disappointed

Name _____

Theme Test
Theme 1

39. When the fire hydrant was opened, water _____ everywhere.

Ⓐ gushed

Ⓑ trudged

Ⓒ modeled

Ⓓ squirmed

40. At the end of the day, the bell rang to _____ the students.

Ⓕ hinder

Ⓖ ponder

Ⓗ dismiss

Ⓘ conquer

41. When she didn't give up, Amy showed that she knew how to _____.

Ⓐ research

Ⓑ camouflage

Ⓒ anticipate

Ⓓ persevere

42. If you work hard, you will _____ your goals.

Ⓕ attain

Ⓖ apply

Ⓗ survive

Ⓘ feature

Robust Vocabulary

GO ON

Name _____

Theme Test
Theme 1

43. The best-selling book was very _____ with children.
    - Ⓐ loyal
    - Ⓑ popular
    - Ⓒ ambitious
    - Ⓓ patchwork

44. When Peter and David wore the same shirt to school it was quite a _____.
    - Ⓕ research
    - Ⓖ donated
    - Ⓗ resistance
    - Ⓘ coincidence

45. Moira believes in herself; she has a lot of _____.
    - Ⓐ media
    - Ⓑ viewers
    - Ⓒ invention
    - Ⓓ confidence

Robust Vocabulary

Name _____

Grammar

Theme Test
Theme 1

▶ **Read and answer Numbers 46 through 55.**

46. Which of these is a complete sentence?
    - (F) The cat ran.
    - (G) To the store.
    - (H) Mary's pet monkey.
    - (I) When David ate the raspberries.

47. Which sentence below should end with a question mark?
    - (A) There are many pigs on this farm
    - (B) People love nice weather
    - (C) Most dogs like to swim
    - (D) Where is he

48. Which of these is a command?
    - (F) Clean your room.
    - (G) My name is Carrie.
    - (H) Vanilla is my favorite.
    - (I) Have you been to the store?

49. Which of these is an exclamation?
    - (A) Kathy loves to run and jump.
    - (B) The dog ate my sandwich.
    - (C) Where are my glasses?
    - (D) Oh, no!

Grammar

GO ON

Name _____

Theme Test
Theme 1

50. Which of these sentences contains a compound subject?
    - F) Mary and Anna collect dolls.
    - G) Peter loves to read comic books.
    - H) Allison hopped, skipped, and jumped.
    - I) Aiden swam across the pool three times.

51. Which of these sentences contains a compound predicate?
    - A) Aaron went home.
    - B) Toby turned and ran.
    - C) Lisa had three hot dogs for lunch.
    - D) Molly and Susan sharpened their pencils.

52. Which of these is a statement?
    - F) Will you join us for dinner?
    - G) I don't like meatballs.
    - H) Be on time.
    - I) Yikes!

53. Which of these is a question?
    - A) I can't wait to see you!
    - B) Don't run in the hallway.
    - C) Catherine rode her bike on Tuesday.
    - D) Have you seen any good movies lately?

Grammar

GO ON

Name _____

Theme Test
Theme 1

54. Which of these sentences is written correctly?

　Ⓕ Tim, Rob, George goes to the fair.

　Ⓖ Li and Pam and Ruth helped the lost boy.

　Ⓗ Cynthia, Heather, and Brenda ate cake at the party.

　Ⓘ Juan and Louis, Willy asked if they could have seconds.

55. Which of these sentences is written correctly?

　Ⓐ When she saw me he smiled and waived hugged me.

　Ⓑ In gym class we hop, gallop, and skip.

　Ⓒ The dog ran jumped and barked.

　Ⓓ Edmund tripped and stumbled fell.

Grammar

Name _____

Theme Test
Theme 1

Writing to a Prompt

> Everyone has learned something that is important.
> Think about a time you learned something important.
> Now write a story about a time when you learned something important.

Planning Page

▶ Use this space to make your notes before you begin writing.
The writing on this page will NOT be scored.

_____
_____
_____
_____
_____
_____
_____
_____
_____
_____

Writing to a Prompt

GO ON

Name _____

Theme Test
Theme 1

▶ **Begin writing here. The writing on this page and the next WILL be scored.**

Writing to a Prompt

Name _____

Theme Test

Theme 1

Writing to a Prompt

Name _____

Theme Test
Theme 1

Oral Reading Fluency

Today was not a regular day at our school. After lunch all of the classes went to the gym for a special program.

When we walked into the gym, we saw a big stage that was covered with cages of all different shapes and sizes. My friends and I wondered, "What is going on?"

After everyone sat down, our teacher announced that the zoo had brought animals for us to see. The people from the zoo began opening the cages. A woman reached into one cage and pulled out a beautiful green and blue parrot. It squawked loudly and flapped its wings. The next animal we saw was a big brown owl with long claws on its feet. The man holding it was wearing thick gloves to protect his skin.

My favorite animal was a baby alligator. It was sitting so still that I thought it was made out of plastic. But all of a sudden, it snapped its jaws and took everyone by surprise. Today was a really fun day at school, and I will remember it for a long time.

Name _____

Theme Test

Theme 1

    What do you want to be when you become an adult? Do you want to be an elementary school teacher? How about a doctor or a police officer? No matter what you want to be, you will need an education to make your dream come true. That is why attending school is so important.

    When you go to school, you learn many skills, such as reading and writing. You also learn about math and science and how to use a computer. Without these skills, you will not be able to get a good job.

    As you study, you will also learn about yourself and what kind of job you might be good at in the future. You will probably discover that some subjects in school are easier for you than others.

    Friends are another important part of school. As you work and play with the others in your classroom, you will make many friends. You will learn how to get along with people, which is another skill that you will need when you grow up.

STORYtown
HARCOURT SCHOOL PUBLISHERS

School Days/Theme 1

Grade 3

Theme Tests

www.harcourtschool.com

Twists and Turns — Theme 2

Name _____ Date _____

Performance Summary

Student Score

READING

Reading Comprehension
    Multiple-Choice Items   _____/18
    Short-Response Open-Ended Item   _____/2
    Extended-Response Open-Ended Item   _____/4

Phonics/Spelling   _____/15

Robust Vocabulary   _____/10

    Total Student Reading Score   _____/49

LANGUAGE ARTS
    Grammar   _____/10

WRITING   _____/6

ORAL READING FLUENCY
    Passage 1   _____ Words Correct Per Minute
    Passage 2   _____ Words Correct Per Minute

(Bubble in the appropriate performance level.)

Reading

Below Basic	Basic (On-Level)	Proficient (On-Level)	Advanced
1–20	21–30	31–40	41–49
○	○	○	○

Language Arts

Below Basic	Basic (On-Level)	Proficient (On-Level)	Advanced
1–4	5–6	7–8	9–10
○	○	○	○

Writing

Below Basic	Basic (On-Level)	Proficient (On-Level)	Advanced
1–2	3–4	5	6
○	○	○	○

Oral Reading Fluency

25th Percentile	50th Percentile	75th Percentile	90th Percentile
44 WCPM	71 WCPM	99 WCPM	128 WCPM
○	○	○	○

For permission to reprint copyrighted material, grateful acknowledgment is made to the following sources:

Highlights for Children, Inc., Columbus, Ohio: "Marmalade" by Betty Bates, illustrated by Bridget Starr Taylor from *Highlights for Children* Magazine, January 2005. Copyright © 2005 by Highlights for Children, Inc. "The Family Tree" by C. R. Harris, illustrated by Valeri Gorbachev from *Highlights for Children* Magazine, February 2002. Copyright © 2002 by Highlights for Children, Inc.

Copyright © by Harcourt, Inc.

All rights reserved. No part of this publication may be reproduced or transmitted in any form or by any means, electronic or mechanical, including photocopy, recording, or any information storage and retrieval system, without permission in writing from the publisher.

Permission is hereby granted to individuals using the corresponding student's textbook or kit as the major vehicle for regular classroom instruction to photocopy entire pages from this publication in classroom quantities for instructional use and not for resale. Requests for information on other matters regarding duplication of this work should be addressed to School Permissions and Copyrights, Harcourt, Inc., 6277 Sea Harbor Drive, Orlando, Florida 32887-6777. Fax: 407-345-2418.

HARCOURT and the Harcourt Logo are trademarks of Harcourt, Inc., registered in the United States of America and/or other jurisdictions.

Printed in the United States of America

ISBN 10 0-15-368492-5
ISBN 13 978-0-15-368492-0 (Package of 12)

9 10   1409   16 15 14 13 12 11 10

If you have received these materials as examination copies free of charge, Harcourt School Publishers retains title to the materials and they may not be resold. Resale of examination copies is strictly prohibited and is illegal.

Possession of this publication in print format does not entitle users to convert this publication, or any portion of it, into electronic format.

Name _____

Theme Test
Theme 2

Reading Comprehension

▶ Read the story "Saving the Butterflies" before answering Numbers 1 through 7.

Saving the Butterflies

Monarch butterflies are a wonder of the world. With their beautiful colors and graceful movements, people love to see these magical insects.

Monarch butterflies travel thousands of miles during their lives. They are born in southern Canada and the United States. In the fall, the young butterflies fly to central Mexico. When warm weather comes, the butterflies fly back north. They will lay their eggs there. This trip is more than 2,000 miles. Imagine how tired you would be if you flew all those miles!

These beautiful butterflies need a plant called milkweed to lay their eggs on. The trouble is, farmers use strong weed killers to protect their crops, and sometimes milkweed is also killed.

Another problem is that people cut down trees that are home to the butterflies. They stay in these trees in the winter. Cutting down the trees leaves the butterflies without a safe home.

But there is good news, too. Monarch butterflies are strong, and they have survived difficult problems in the past. Scientists in the United States, Canada, and Mexico are working together to help the monarchs. They are trying to protect the milkweed plants and the forests. Scientists believe we should have a world full of monarch butterflies.

Reading Comprehension

Name _____

▶ Now answer Numbers 1 through 7. Base your answers on the story "Saving the Butterflies."

1. Read this sentence from the story.

   With their beautiful colors and graceful movements, people love to see these magical insects.

   Which word means the OPPOSITE of *graceful*?
   Ⓐ bright
   Ⓑ strong
   Ⓒ clumsy
   Ⓓ ugly

2. Which of the following is an OPINION and not a fact?
   Ⓕ Scientists are working to help butterflies.
   Ⓖ Farmers should not kill milkweed plants.
   Ⓗ Butterflies fly more than 2,000 miles.
   Ⓘ Butterflies live in trees in winter.

3. Which of these is the BEST reference source to learn more about monarch butterflies?
   Ⓐ atlas
   Ⓑ dictionary
   Ⓒ thesaurus
   Ⓓ encyclopedia

Reading Comprehension   2   GO ON

© Harcourt • Grade 3

Name _____

Theme Test
Theme 2

4. According to the article, where do monarch butterflies lay their eggs?
    - (F) on tree branches
    - (G) in the grass
    - (H) under water
    - (I) on milkweed plants

5. Which of these is a FACT and not an opinion?
    - (A) Butterflies are beautiful.
    - (B) Butterflies should be protected.
    - (C) Butterflies travel a long way.
    - (D) Butterflies are magical creatures.

6. Which of these is the BEST reference source to use to learn more about milkweed?
    - (F) atlas
    - (G) dictionary
    - (H) math textbook
    - (I) thesaurus

Reading Comprehension

GO ON

Name _____

Theme Test
Theme 2

7. The article tells about two problems monarch butterflies face. Choose one of these problems and describe a possible solution. Use information and details from the article to support your answer.

_____
_____
_____
_____
_____
_____
_____
_____
_____
_____
_____

Reading Comprehension

GO ON

Name _____

Theme Test
Theme 2

▶ Read the story "Who Will Clean up the Park?" before answering Numbers 8 through 13.

Who Will Clean up the Park?

Antonio sat on a bench in his neighborhood park and looked around. A year ago, the park had been clean and nice. It was a fun place to visit. Families liked to have picnics there, and children liked to play on the playground and feed the ducks.

Now the once-beautiful park was dirty. Empty soda cans and bottles littered the grass. Candy wrappers were scattered in the wood chips under the playground. There were broken toys in the sandbox, and there was an unpleasant smell near the trash cans. There was even trash floating in the duck pond. Antonio felt disgusted.

Antonio walked over to his friend Anita, who was playing near the swings. "Do you remember what our park used to look like?" he asked her.

Anita looked up at Antonio and frowned. "It used to be so pretty," she said. "Now it looks like no one cares about it. I wish we could do something to help, but I don't think the two of us can clean up this whole park."

Antonio thought for a moment, his eyes scanning the park. "Maybe there is something we can do to help," he said. "I know people from the neighborhood would help us clean it up if we asked them. I know my parents would help out, and I'm sure yours would, too."

"I have an idea," said Anita. "I love to draw. I can make some posters to show people how much the park means to us and how they can help us keep it clean and safe. I know my brother will want to help, too."

"Good idea," Antonio said, excitedly. "Maybe we can put up posters at school and around the neighborhood, asking people to come and help. I'll talk to other kids at school and ask them to meet us here next Saturday. If we all work together, it won't take long to get the park cleaned up. Then more people will want to bring their families to visit it.

Reading Comprehension

GO ON

If everyone remembers how important it is to keep our park clean, it won't ever look like this again."

Anita nodded her head enthusiastically. "I'll get started on the posters as soon as I get home," she said. "I can't wait to see our park looking pretty again!"

Name _____

Theme Test
Theme 2

▶ Now answer Numbers 8 through 13. Base your answers on the story "Who Will Clean up the Park?"

8. Which words from the story have almost the same meaning?
   Ⓐ park, picnic
   Ⓑ littered, scattered
   Ⓒ frowned, nodded
   Ⓓ pretty, disgusted

9. What is the main idea of this story?
   Ⓕ Posters are a good way to share important ideas.
   Ⓖ Working together can help solve a problem.
   Ⓗ Ducks should not swim in dirty water.
   Ⓘ Parks are a fun place to play.

10. What does Antonio see in the sandbox?
    Ⓐ candy wrappers
    Ⓑ empty bottles
    Ⓒ broken toys
    Ⓓ soda cans

11. Which of the following is an OPINION and not a fact?
    Ⓕ The park had been clean in the past.
    Ⓖ There is trash by the swings.
    Ⓗ Food should not be allowed in the park.
    Ⓘ People had come to the park for picnics.

Reading Comprehension

GO ON

Name _____

Theme Test
Theme 2

12. What is the BEST reference source to find out information about a park near you?

Ⓐ atlas
Ⓑ Internet
Ⓒ thesaurus
Ⓓ dictionary

READ THINK EXPLAIN

13. This story has two characters, Antonio and Anita. What two characteristics do Antonio and Anita share? Use information and details from the story to support your answer.

_____
_____
_____
_____
_____
_____
_____

Reading Comprehension

GO ON

Read the story "Marmalade" before answering Numbers 14 through 20.

Marmalade

by Betty Bates

Illustrated by Bridget Starr Taylor

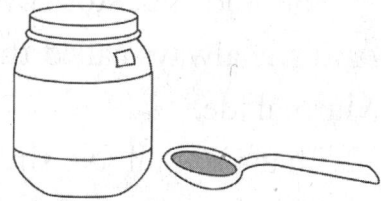

Every once in a while my great-uncle Waldo gets into a reminiscing mode. This morning it happened at breakfast. He picked up a knife with his knuckly fingers, spread marmalade on his toast, gave a chuckle, and began:

Whenever I spread marmalade, I think of my mother. She was a wonderful woman, a five-foot-tall good person.

She even befriended a skunk.

One day she was out back picking beans when she turned to see a skunk no more than a yard away. Well sir, do you think she panicked? Think she worried that the creature would spray his scent all over her and the beans?

She did not.

There was a reason for that. You see, this skunk had a marmalade jar stuck on his nose. Mother sort of smiled at that little wild thing. But the skunk just turned his head to one side and looked pitiful.

Of course, his predicament served him right. There was no question that he'd been rummaging around in someone's garbage.

Even so, Mother took pity on him. Still on her knees, she inched across the grass, reached out, and twisted the jar—very carefully.

The jar slid off. The skunk nodded a thank-you, then turned and slipped into the woods at the back of the garden. None of this spraying business. Not on my wonderful mother.

Mother took pity on him.

Reading Comprehension

GO ON

She told that story over and over. And she always called the skunk Marmalade.

That's not all. No sir. There was the time, maybe three summers later, when I was about twelve.

It was a rainy morning. Dad went to work, and Mother went shopping. My friend Rob came over so we could run the electric train in my room. All of a sudden, a scratching sound came from the attic.

"Sounds like some kind of animal," Rob said.

"Yeah. Let's take a look."

What was I thinking? It could have been a wolf!

Out in the hall, I opened the attic door—very slowly. The noise stopped. I climbed a few steps. My eyes were at floor level. I saw nothing but boxes and trunks and an old dollhouse.

I climbed to the top of the stairs with Rob after me.

Silence.

"Let's look around," I said.

I found the animal behind a carton near the chimney. You guessed it. Black with a white stripe down its back. Was he scared and shivering? You bet. At least that's how I remember it.

I backed away. Would he spray me? Do skunks bite?

"Hey, Rob. I found him. Let's go figure out a plan to get him out of here."

We scrambled down the steps.

"It's a skunk," I said. "It might even be Marmalade."

"Marmalade?"

I explained.

"Funny name for a skunk," Rob said. "*Marmalade.*"

I snapped my fingers. That could be the answer. But was this really the same skunk? Would he remember?

"Come on," I said. "Let's go to the kitchen."

In the cupboard we found Mother's custard cups. We dumped a teaspoon of marmalade into each one. We set one on the back porch, one just inside the back door, and one every few feet all the way up to the attic.

Then, very carefully, I set the last one in front of the skunk.

I backed away.

The skunk sniffed. He inched forward. He licked the cup. He ate the marmalade.

Rob and I followed as Marmalade ate his way down two flights of stairs, through the kitchen, and out to the porch.

When he was through gobbling his last bit of marmalade, he turned and looked at us. What was he going to do?

He stared for a long time. And then, finally, he gave us a big toothy grin before scampering away into the rain.

He remembered my mother's kindness, all right.

Would he remember?

Name _____

▶ **Now answer Numbers 14 through 20. Base your answers on the story "Marmalade."**

14. Why does great-uncle Waldo start to tell the story about the skunk?
    Ⓕ He sees a skunk.
    Ⓖ He is cleaning out his attic.
    Ⓗ He smells the spray of a skunk.
    Ⓘ He is spreading marmalade on toast.

15. What is the MAIN idea of this story?
    Ⓐ Watch out for skunks.
    Ⓑ It is fun to tell stories about the past.
    Ⓒ Skunks like to go through people's trash.
    Ⓓ Animals remember how they have been treated.

16. What is the BEST reference source to find out information about what skunks like to eat?
    Ⓕ an atlas
    Ⓖ a thesaurus
    Ⓗ a town newspaper
    Ⓘ a book about forest animals

Reading Comprehension

Name _____

Theme Test
Theme 2

17. Read this sentence from the story.

> **Every once in a while my great-uncle Waldo gets into a reminiscing mode.**

Which word means almost the SAME as *reminiscing*?

Ⓐ crying

Ⓑ laughing

Ⓒ remembering

Ⓓ persuading

18. Which of the following is an OPINION and not a fact?

Ⓕ Skunks are scary.

Ⓖ Skunks like marmalade.

Ⓗ Great-uncle Waldo likes to tell stories.

Ⓘ Great-uncle Waldo had a friend named Rob.

19. Where in the attic do the boys find the skunk?

Ⓐ in a dollhouse

Ⓑ in the trash can

Ⓒ under a trunk

Ⓓ behind a carton

20. Read this sentence from the story.

> **And then, finally, he gave us a big toothy grin before scampering away into the rain.**

Which word means almost the OPPOSITE of *scampering*?

Ⓕ strolling

Ⓖ running

Ⓗ hopping

Ⓘ dashing

Reading Comprehension
13
STOP

Name _____

Phonics/Spelling

Theme Test
Theme 2

▶ For Numbers 21 through 24, choose the best answer for each question.

21. How should you divide the word <u>playground</u> into two words?

    (A) pla-yground
    (B) play-ground
    (C) pl-ayground
    (D) playgro-und

22. How should you divide the word <u>catfish</u> into two words?

    (F) cat-fish
    (G) ca-tfish
    (H) catf-ish
    (I) catfi-sh

23. How should you divide the word <u>chalkboard</u> into two words?

    (A) ch-alkboard
    (B) chal-kboard
    (C) chalkb-oard
    (D) chalk-board

24. How should you divide the word <u>butterfly</u> into two words?

    (F) but-terfly
    (G) bu-tterfly
    (H) butter-fly
    (I) butterf-ly

Phonics/Spelling

Name _____

Theme Test
Theme 2

▶ For Numbers 25 through 35, read each model word. Then fill in the circle next to the word that has the same sound as the underlined part of the model word and correctly completes each sentence.

25. mat<u>ch</u>

   The boy is learning how to _____.

   Ⓐ run
   Ⓑ catch
   Ⓒ rich
   Ⓓ conquer

26. <u>ch</u>alk

   I didn't have time to stand around and _____.

   Ⓕ chat
   Ⓖ talk
   Ⓗ argue
   Ⓘ sharp

27. j<u>oi</u>n

   I can't stand the _____.

   Ⓐ loyal
   Ⓑ mess
   Ⓒ noise
   Ⓓ taste

Phonics/Spelling   15   **GO ON**

Name _____

Theme Test

Theme 2

28. <u>hou</u>se

   Did you see the little _____?

   Ⓕ tow

   Ⓖ baby

   Ⓗ mouse

   Ⓘ hamster

29. t<u>oy</u>

   Do not _____ your brother.

   Ⓐ bother

   Ⓑ toil

   Ⓒ annoy

   Ⓓ copy

30. <u>wh</u>eat

   The car was missing a _____.

   Ⓕ wire

   Ⓖ seat

   Ⓗ horn

   Ⓘ wheel

31. w<u>ow</u>

   The farmer has a horse and a _____.

   Ⓐ slow

   Ⓑ cow

   Ⓒ house

   Ⓓ sheep

Phonics/Spelling

GO ON

Name _____

Theme Test
Theme 2

32. short

He chose a _____ for the party.

Ⓕ chin
Ⓖ tiger
Ⓗ shirt
Ⓘ sandwich

33. scram

He fell and _____ his knee.

Ⓐ hit
Ⓑ screamed
Ⓒ broke
Ⓓ scraped

34. strap

Draw a _____ line.

Ⓕ strong
Ⓖ black
Ⓗ straight
Ⓘ squiggly

35. spry

Ellen's favorite season is _____.

Ⓐ spring
Ⓑ June
Ⓒ fall
Ⓓ sprain

Phonics/Spelling

17

STOP

© Harcourt • Grade 3

Name _____

Robust Vocabulary

Theme Test
Theme 2

▶ Choose the best word to complete each sentence for Numbers 36 through 45.

36. The couch was old and _____.
    - F) dazed
    - G) shabby
    - H) elevated
    - I) generous

37. There was very little to eat during the _____.
    - A) patrol
    - B) midst
    - C) famine
    - D) contribution

38. Curious about the missing keys, Diane decided to _____.
    - F) obey
    - G) babble
    - H) investigate
    - I) communicate

39. The ball rolled faster and faster, building _____ as it went.
    - A) scent
    - B) chatter
    - C) initiative
    - D) momentum

Robust Vocabulary

Name _____

40. When I came into the room, she was awake and _____.

- (F) alert
- (G) dominant
- (H) competent
- (I) perplexed

41. Rhonda likes to explore new things; she is very _____.

- (A) suspicious
- (B) inquisitive
- (C) ferocious
- (D) agreeable

42. Because he had read a lot about them, Paul was an _____ about birds.

- (F) expert
- (G) obey
- (H) alert
- (I) initiative

43. Rosa bought the _____ for a recipe at the grocery store.

- (A) ingredients
- (B) scents
- (C) laboratories
- (D) signals

44. Lori likes to _____ out the window.
    F demonstrate
    G suspect
    H confess
    I gaze

45. The store had many balloons in _____ colors.
    A wanders
    B various
    C charging
    D disappointed

Grammar

▶ **Read and answer Numbers 46 through 55.**

46. Which of these is a complete sentence?

    Ⓕ At the store.

    Ⓖ And the baby.

    Ⓗ Marcus runs fast.

    Ⓘ When Maurice rode his bike.

47. Which of these is a compound sentence?

    Ⓐ She went to the store.

    Ⓑ She got one, and so did I.

    Ⓒ Kathy likes to sing and dance.

    Ⓓ Travis likes dogs, cats, and rabbits.

48. Which of these is the correct way to combine the following sentences?

    I run.

    I jump.

    Ⓕ I run jump.

    Ⓖ I run I jump.

    Ⓗ I run, jump.

    Ⓘ I run and jump.

49. Which of these is a noun?

    Ⓐ red

    Ⓑ fell

    Ⓒ apple

    Ⓓ running

Name _____

Theme Test
Theme 2

50. Which of these is a proper noun?
   - F candy
   - G monkey
   - H Mexico
   - I flower

51. Which of these is written correctly?
   - A Mrr.
   - B Mrs.
   - C Doc.
   - D Mss.

52. Which of these sentences is written correctly?
   - F The abbreviation for Ohio is OH.
   - G The abbreviation for Maine is Me.
   - H The abbreviation for Indiana is iN.
   - I The abbreviation for California is ca.

53. Which of these shows the plural form of house?
   - A house
   - B houses
   - C housses
   - D housees

Grammar

GO ON

Name _____

Theme Test
Theme 2

54. Which of these shows the correct singular and plural forms?

    Ⓕ mouse, mouses

    Ⓖ fork, forks

    Ⓗ city, citys

    Ⓘ ant, antes

55. Which of these is the correct plural form of baby?

    Ⓐ baby

    Ⓑ babys

    Ⓒ babyes

    Ⓓ babies

Grammar

Name _____

Writing to a Prompt

Theme Test
Theme 2

▶ Read the story "The Family Tree" before responding to the prompt following the story.

The Family Tree
by C.R. Harris
illustrated by Valeri Gorbachev

In Windy Wood, the Family Tree had stood proud and tall for many years.

The Squirrel family stored nuts beneath its roots. The Woodpecker family pecked insects from its trunk. The Crow family built nests in its topmost branches.

Then one day, Owl came flying by with a warning. "Hoo-hoo!" he hooted, "The woodcutters are coming!"

"What's that you say?" asked Grandmother Squirrel. Then she heard the noise: RRRRRR! "TIMBER!"

CRAAAA—SH!

"No, don't tell me!" she chattered. "It's those woodcutters with their saws, taking trees from Windy Wood. Maybe this is the year when they'll cut down our tree!"

Straight down the knobby old tree trunk she scurried. "Stop!" she called to her grandchildren. "Don't store any more nuts down here. If the Family Tree is cut down, they'll be lost."

RRRRRR! "TIMBER!" CRAAAAAA—SH!

The Woodpecker brothers shook their heads. "Listen," they said. "That crash was louder than the last one. The woodcutters are coming closer. What will we do if they drag the Family Tree away? We've always pecked insects out of its trunk. Our parents pecked insects out. So did their parents. And their parents before them."

RRRRR! "TIMBER!" CRAAAAAAA—SH!

"That was the loudest crash of all," cawed Mother Crow, flapping her wings. "All of you are worrying over nothing. There are hundreds more hidey-holes for nuts in Windy Wood. There are thousands more insects to peck out of other tree trunks."

She shook her head sadly. "But what will happen to me if the woodcutters cut down the Family Tree? I'll tell you what will happen. My nest will come crashing down, and my poor babies will come down with it!"

"Maybe the woodcutters won't come any nearer," said Owl. "I've been watching how they choose which trees to cut down. This is what happens. One woodcutter carries a bucket of paint. He paints a red cross on each tree that's to be cut."

"Oh no!" cawed Mother Crow, looking through the trees. "Here he comes now!" Bravely, she dived at the woodcutter's head, calling, "Keep away from my babies! Keep away!"

"He can't understand you," Owl told her sadly. "Woodcutters are humans. And humans can't understand what we birds and animals say."

The woodcutter dipped his brush into the bucket of red paint. All the squirrels and woodpeckers and crows gathered to watch.

They saw him stare at the old tree they all loved so much. Then suddenly he called to the other woodcutters, "Come and look at the names carved into this tree trunk! That's my pa's name, and my ma's. That date underneath is the year they got married."

"Come and look!"

He shook his head. "We're not cutting down *this* tree, guys. This is my Family Tree."

Name _____

Theme Test
Theme 2

> In "The Family Tree," many of the animals were afraid that their family tree would be cut down.
> Think about how they must have felt when the tree was not cut down. Now write to explain how the animals felt once they knew that the tree would not be cut down.

Planning Page

▶ Use this space to make your notes before you begin writing. The writing on this page will NOT be scored.

_____
_____
_____
_____
_____
_____
_____
_____
_____
_____
_____
_____

Writing to a Prompt

Name _____

Theme Test
Theme 2

▶ Begin writing here. The writing on this page and the next WILL be scored.

Writing to a Prompt

Name _____

Theme Test
Theme 2

_____

_____

_____

_____

_____

_____

_____

_____

_____

_____

_____

_____

_____

_____

_____

_____

Writing to a Prompt

Oral Reading Fluency

It was the first snowy day of winter. Bob walked outside to shovel his sidewalk. The snow had been falling all night, and it was already about six inches deep. When Bob was about halfway finished with his part of the sidewalk, his arms began to ache.

He took a break from shoveling and peered across the street. He waved to his friends who were outside working, too. Then he noticed that the woman everyone in the neighborhood called "Grandma" was outside shoveling her sidewalk alone.

"Guys!" he shouted, "Let's pitch in and help Grandma clear away the mess on her sidewalk!"

All of Bob's friends rushed to Grandma's part of the sidewalk and began shoveling as quickly as they could. Grandma watched the boys shoveling with tears in her eyes. She was very grateful for their help. "Would you come to my house for hot chocolate when you're finished working?" she asked them. They all agreed. Later that day, they learned that Grandma made the best hot chocolate in town.

You probably have chores that you do at home. But do you have a responsibility to keep the town where you live running smoothly? If you lived in Nigeria, you probably would.

Nigeria is a country in Africa. Most people in Nigeria live in small villages. The people work hard to keep their villages clean and safe. In order to make sure that all of the work is finished, each individual has a job to do. The people of each village are divided into groups by age. Each age group works together to complete its job. Working together makes the job fun.

Groups of young children sweep the village and keep it clean. A group of adults is in charge of keeping the water the village uses for drinking and bathing clean. Other groups build houses and roads. The oldest members of the community share stories about the past and give advice to younger people.

Because everyone belongs to a group, everyone knows what job to do. The work gets done quickly, and everyone becomes closer to the other members of the community.

HARCOURT SCHOOL PUBLISHERS
STORYtown

Together We Can/Theme 2

Grade 3

Theme Tests

Harcourt
SCHOOL PUBLISHERS

www.harcourtschool.com

ISBN-13: 978-0-15-358755-9
ISBN-10: 0-15-358755-5

Twists and Turns — Theme 3

Name _____ Date _____

Performance Summary

Student Score

READING

Reading Comprehension
    Multiple-Choice Items   _____/18
    Short-Response Open-Ended Item   _____/2
    Extended-Response Open-Ended Item   _____/4

Phonics/Spelling   _____/15

Robust Vocabulary   _____/10

    Total Student Reading Score   _____/**49**

LANGUAGE ARTS
    Grammar   _____/10

WRITING   _____/6

ORAL READING FLUENCY
    Passage 1   _____ Words Correct Per Minute
    Passage 2   _____ Words Correct Per Minute

(Bubble in the appropriate performance level.)

Reading

Below Basic	Basic (On-Level)	Proficient (On-Level)	Advanced
1–20	21–30	31–40	41–49
○	○	○	○

Language Arts

Below Basic	Basic (On-Level)	Proficient (On-Level)	Advanced
1–4	5–6	7–8	9–10
○	○	○	○

Writing

Below Basic	Basic (On-Level)	Proficient (On-Level)	Advanced
1–2	3–4	5	6
○	○	○	○

Oral Reading Fluency

25th Percentile	50th Percentile	75th Percentile	90th Percentile
62 WCPM	92 WCPM	120 WCPM	146 WCPM
○	○	○	○

Grateful acknowledgment is made to Bayard Presse Canada Inc. for permission to reprint/adapt from "Big Foot Goes Ice Fishing" by Michael Arvaarluk Kusugak, illustrated by Jean Morin in *chickaDEE* Magazine, December 1999.

Copyright © by Harcourt, Inc.

All rights reserved. No part of this publication may be reproduced or transmitted in any form or by any means, electronic or mechanical, including photocopy, recording, or any information storage and retrieval system, without permission in writing from the publisher.

Permission is hereby granted to individuals using the corresponding student's textbook or kit as the major vehicle for regular classroom instruction to photocopy entire pages from this publication in classroom quantities for instructional use and not for resale. Requests for information on other matters regarding duplication of this work should be addressed to School Permissions and Copyrights, Harcourt, Inc., 6277 Sea Harbor Drive, Orlando, Florida 32887-6777. Fax: 407-345-2418.

HARCOURT and the Harcourt Logo are trademarks of Harcourt, Inc., registered in the United States of America and/or other jurisdictions.

Printed in the United States of America

ISBN 10 0-15-358755-5
ISBN 13 978-0-15-358755-9 (Package of 12)

9 10 1409 16 15 14 13 12 11 10

If you have received these materials as examination copies free of charge, Harcourt School Publishers retains title to the materials and they may not be resold. Resale of examination copies is strictly prohibited and is illegal.

Possession of this publication in print format does not entitle users to convert this publication, or any portion of it, into electronic format.

Name _____

Reading Comprehension

Theme Test
Theme 3

▶ Read the story "Friends Forever?" before answering Numbers 1 through 6.

Friends Forever?

Rita and Paula had been best friends since first grade. Now, both girls were running for third grade president. Each girl made a campaign speech and put up posters. Each girl was hard at work to get enough votes to win.

As a result, things were not the same between the two girls. There were three third grade classes, and they only got together at recess, lunch, and gym. Whenever the two girls saw each other, they didn't greet one another or talk together.

Still, the job of president was so much fun that it was worth going for. Students and teachers worked together on plays and fund-raising projects, and the president led the students who took part.

By the end of the day on Friday, all the votes had been counted. Paula had 42 votes and Rita had 35. Rita was disappointed, but she congratulated Paula anyway. Paula said she hoped they could stay best friends. Rita shook her hand and agreed.

That was easier said than done. Paula ate lunch with new kids, and Rita didn't call Paula at night anymore to share the things that had happened to her during the day. It was hard for Rita to get over her jealousy that Paula won the election.

As the weeks passed, Rita and Paula learned how to get along without each other. Maybe in the future they would be best friends again. In the meantime, they smiled at each other in the hallways as they walked with new friends.

Reading Comprehension

GO ON

Name _____

Theme Test
Theme 3

▶ Now answer Numbers 1 through 6. Base your answers on the story "Friends Forever?".

1. Which of the following happened as a result of the election?
    - Ⓐ Students worked together.
    - Ⓑ Paula ate lunch with new kids.
    - Ⓒ Rita and Paula became best friends.
    - Ⓓ There were three third grade classes.

2. Read the sentence from the story.

    > It was hard for Rita to get over her jealousy that Paula won the election.

    What word has almost the SAME meaning as *jealousy*?
    - Ⓕ envy
    - Ⓖ anger
    - Ⓗ excitement
    - Ⓘ disappointment

3. Why did Rita and Paula both run for president?
    - Ⓐ All third graders had to run.
    - Ⓑ They did not like each other.
    - Ⓒ Each wanted to make new friends.
    - Ⓓ The president got to do a lot of fun things.

4. Which of the following would be the BEST source of information about student elections?
    - Ⓕ an atlas
    - Ⓖ a dictionary
    - Ⓗ a science book
    - Ⓘ a school newspaper

Reading Comprehension

GO ON

Name _____

Theme Test
Theme 3

5. Why did the author write "Friends Forever?"
   Ⓐ to explain that friendship isn't always easy
   Ⓑ to persuade readers to make new friends
   Ⓒ to convince readers not to run for office
   Ⓓ to make readers laugh

6. What does the author want the reader to know about friendship? Use details and information from the story to explain your answer.

_____
_____
_____
_____
_____
_____
_____
_____
_____
_____

Reading Comprehension   3   **GO ON**

Name _____

Theme Test
Theme 3

▶ Read the story "The Living English Language" before answering Numbers 7 through 13.

The Living English Language

The English language is a living language. The meanings of words change over time as old words take on new meanings. As computers and the Internet have grown more and more a part of life, several old words have taken on new meanings. The interesting thing about these words is that they have already been around, and they are still in use. But, now they have new meanings as well.

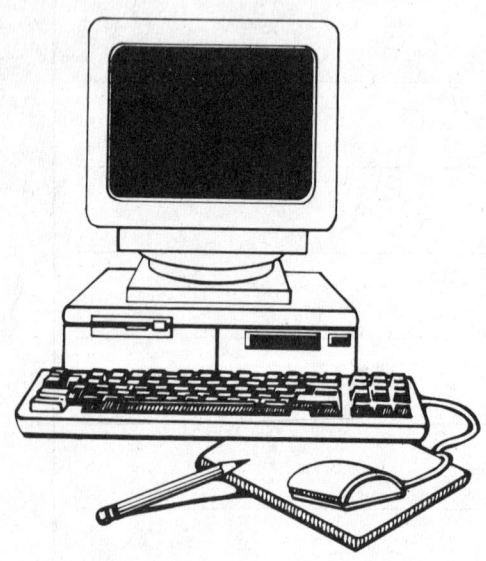

What do you think of when someone says they see a mouse? Do you think of a furry gray rodent with a long tail? Or do you think of the part of the computer that allows you to move quickly from place to place through a document? You can see how the meaning of that one word has changed.

Suppose you hear that something has crashed. Do you think a dish has fallen off the shelf or a friend has fallen off a bike? Do you think about a crash that caused a traffic jam on the news? Maybe you think that someone's computer has stopped working?

What's a program? Is it something you watch on television? Is it something they give you before a play? Or is it something that you install to make your computer work in a new way?

Reading Comprehension

This makes it very important to listen when someone speaks. You want to make sure you know which meaning they mean. In each case you might be right either way, right?

One Word, Many Meanings

Word	Meanings
drive	1) to move by force; 2) to guide the movement of something; 3) to hit a golf ball; 4) the part of a computer that reads and writes data
key	1) a small piece of metal used to open a lock; 2) a list of correct answers; 3) a button on a computer keyboard
mouse	1) a small furry rodent; 2) a shy person; 3) a small device with a button used to control a computer
monitor	1) to watch carefully; 2) a person who watches over others; 3) the screen of a computer

Name _____

Theme Test
Theme 3

▶ Now answer Numbers 7 through 13. Base your answers on the story "The Living English Language."

7. What is this article MOSTLY about?
   - Ⓕ reading
   - Ⓖ language
   - Ⓗ programs
   - Ⓘ computers

8. Why did the author write "The Living English Language?"
   - Ⓐ to inform readers about how language changes
   - Ⓑ to discourage readers from using the Internet
   - Ⓒ to encourage people to read more books
   - Ⓓ to compare different meanings of *crash*

9. Why does the author say it is important to listen when someone talks?
   - Ⓕ so you won't be rude
   - Ⓖ so you don't need to ask questions
   - Ⓗ so you know which word meaning is meant
   - Ⓘ so you can understand how language grows

10. According to the chart, what would you need if you wanted to save data on your computer?
    - Ⓐ a key
    - Ⓑ a drive
    - Ⓒ a mouse
    - Ⓓ a monitor

Reading Comprehension

6

GO ON

© Harcourt • Grade 3

Name _____

Theme Test
Theme 3

11. According to the chart, what word describes a shy person?

- Ⓕ key
- Ⓖ drive
- Ⓗ mouse
- Ⓘ monitor

12. According to the chart, which of the following is a meaning of *drive*?

- Ⓐ a small furry rodent
- Ⓑ to watch carefully
- Ⓒ to hit a golf ball
- Ⓓ a shy person

READ THINK EXPLAIN

13. The article explains how language has changed with the invention and use of computers. Using information from the article, choose one word, and explain its different meanings.

_____

_____

_____

_____

_____

_____

Reading Comprehension

GO ON

Read the story "Big Foot Goes Ice Fishing" before answering Numbers 14 through 20.

Big Foot Goes Ice Fishing

by Michael Arvaarluk Kusugak

"Dad?" Silu said.

"Yes, Irniik," said his father. Irniik means son in Inuktitut.

"How come the ice chisel does not float?" Silu asked. Silu was 8 years old and always asking questions.

"Because it is too heavy," his father replied.

"But it is made of wood and wood floats," Silu said.

"The chisel part is very heavy metal and the wood handle is hard and heavy so it will not float," his father said. "Now where is it?"

"It is in that hole," Silu said, pointing to a fishing hole.

"Oh no! You dropped the ice chisel in the hole?" his father asked.

Silu said, "I thought it might float."

Silu and his father were ice fishing at Peter Lake near Rankin Inlet. After the cold of winter begins to leave the land and the sun begins to soften the ice, people from all over Nunavut travel there by snowmobile to ice fish for lake trout.

Silu and his father had left home early that morning pulling their sled behind them. When they arrived, they stopped their snowmobile in the middle of the frozen lake. Silu's father made two fishing holes in the ice, one for Silu and one for himself.

Reading Comprehension

GO ON

To make the holes, he cleared the snow, then broke the ice with the chisel to get to the cold water below.

But Silu was not interested in sitting at his hole, jigging a fishing line up and down through the ice, waiting for fish to bite.

There were always more interesting things to do than that. One of those interesting things was to see if the ice chisel would float. And he found out it didn't.

"Well," Silu's father said. "I guess we will not be making any more holes today. Go see if you can catch a fish."

"You're not mad?" Silu asked.

His father laughed. "Well, I'm not really mad, but I will have to make another ice chisel when we get home. You won't drop the next one down a hole, will you?"

"No, Dad," Silu said, smiling a bit.

"Well then, go catch us the biggest trout in this lake!"

"Okay, Dad."

Silu trudged off to his fishing hole. Before long he was back again.

"My feet are cold," he said.

His father said, "No wonder your feet are cold. They're soaking wet. How did that happen?"

"I stuck them into the fishing hole," Silu said.

"Why did you do that?" his father was really surprised.

Silu said, "I wanted to see if my boots were waterproof."

"Why did you think your boots were waterproof?" his father asked.

"Your boots are waterproof, Dad," Silu said.

"My boots are made of sealskin; yours are made of cloth, Silu," he said. "Later we will ask your mother to make you sealskin boots."

"Now, we'd better do something about your cold feet," he said. "Here. You can wear my big slippers."

His father always brought a pair of big sheepskin slippers with ties on the tops of them, that he slipped over his boots when the weather was really cold. Now he took them out of his clothing sack for Silu.

"I can't wear your slippers," Silu said. "They're too big."

"But they'll keep you warm," his father said.

Silu's father took Silu's wet boots off, warmed his son's feet with his big warms hands and put the big, slippers on him. "Now we can call you Big Foot," he said.

Then they drank hot sugary tea and ate bannock, a kind of yummy pancake, that Silu's mother had made. It didn't take long for Silu's feet to warm up.

Afterwards, they went back to fishing. Silu did not fish for long before he was back again at his father's side.

"Now what, Silu?"

"My hook is stuck."

His father went over to Silu's fishing hole. Sure enough the hook was stuck. His father pulled and pulled on the line. He jiggled the line and pulled some more. Eventually, he pulled the hook right out of the hole. Attached to the hook was the ice chisel. Silu's line had hooked onto the ice chisel!

Silu and his father laughed and laughed and laughed some more.

"This is the oddest thing I have ever seen," he said. "You are really lucky, Big Foot."

Silu sat with his father on the snowmobile on the way home, smiling all the way. When they got home they would watch the big hockey game on TV between Toronto and Montreal. And of course, now Silu had a great ice fishing story to tell.

Name _____

Theme Test
Theme 3

▶ Now answer Numbers 14 through 20. Base your answers on the story "Big Foot Goes Ice Fishing."

14. Why does Silu drop the ice chisel in the fishing hole?
    - Ⓕ He is mad at his father.
    - Ⓖ He wants to see if it will float.
    - Ⓗ He wonders if it is waterproof.
    - Ⓘ He hopes it will make a big splash.

15. Read the sentence from the story.

    "The chisel part is very heavy metal and the wood handle is hard and heavy so it will not float," his father said.

    Which word has almost the SAME description as *chisel*?
    - Ⓐ sled
    - Ⓑ shoe
    - Ⓒ hook
    - Ⓓ hammer

16. Why did the author write "Big Foot Goes Ice Fishing?"
    - Ⓕ to teach readers a lesson about manners
    - Ⓖ to alert readers to the dangers of ice fishing
    - Ⓗ to show that accidents can lead to great stories
    - Ⓘ to explain why fathers and sons often disagree

17. Where does this story MOSTLY take place?
    - Ⓐ Peter Lake
    - Ⓑ Rankin Inlet
    - Ⓒ a hockey game
    - Ⓓ a hut made of ice

Reading Comprehension

GO ON

Name _____

Theme Test
Theme 3

18. How did Silu's hook become stuck?

　Ⓕ It was caught in the ice.

　Ⓖ It had hooked a big fish.

　Ⓗ It became attached to the ice chisel.

　Ⓘ It was trapped under the snowmobile.

19. What do Silu and his father eat?

　Ⓐ fish

　Ⓑ hot soup

　Ⓒ pancakes

　Ⓓ sandwiches

20. Why does Silu need sealskin boots?

　Ⓕ His boots are lost.

　Ⓖ His boots are too small.

　Ⓗ His boots are uncomfortable.

　Ⓘ His boots are not waterproof.

Name _____

Phonics/Spelling

Theme Test
Theme 3

▶ Read each sentence that has a blank in it where a word is missing. Choose the correct form of the word to complete the sentence.

21. I like to ride my _____.

   Ⓐ bicycle
   Ⓑ bicykel
   Ⓒ bisickle
   Ⓓ bicickell

22. She blew out the _____.

   Ⓕ candl
   Ⓖ candle
   Ⓗ candel
   Ⓘ candell

23. I fell and twisted my _____.

   Ⓐ ancle
   Ⓑ ankle
   Ⓒ ankel
   Ⓓ anckel

24. After a while, the cookie began to _____.

   Ⓕ crumbell
   Ⓖ crumbel
   Ⓗ crumble
   Ⓘ crumbl

Phonics/Spelling

GO ON

Name _____

Theme Test
Theme 3

▶ **For Numbers 25 through 35, read each model word. Choose the word that has the same sound as the underlined part of the model word and correctly completes each sentence.**

25. k<u>n</u>ot

   The horse belonged to the _____.

   Ⓐ knight
   Ⓑ nickel
   Ⓒ king
   Ⓓ knife

26. <u>wr</u>ong

   The boy _____ on his paper.

   Ⓕ drew
   Ⓖ wrote
   Ⓗ painted
   Ⓘ rained

27. cou<u>gh</u>

   The bark of the tree was _____.

   Ⓐ brown
   Ⓑ gruff
   Ⓒ laugh
   Ⓓ rough

Phonics/Spelling

GO ON

Name _____

Theme Test
Theme 3

28. <u>gn</u>at

We read a story about an elf and a _____.

Ⓕ fairy

Ⓖ nurse

Ⓗ gnome

Ⓘ monster

29. e<u>dg</u>e

The woman was praised for her _____.

Ⓐ effort

Ⓑ stage

Ⓒ patience

Ⓓ knowledge

30. ca<u>g</u>e

She was told not to write in the _____.

Ⓕ margin

Ⓖ book

Ⓗ class

Ⓘ badge

31. <u>c</u>ity

The teacher asked him to draw a _____.

Ⓐ truck

Ⓑ sundae

Ⓒ circle

Ⓓ square

Phonics/Spelling

16

GO ON

© Harcourt • Grade 3

Name _____

Theme Test
Theme 3

32. What is the last syllable of *open*?
    - F) n
    - G) en
    - H) pen
    - I) open

33. What is the first syllable of *beside*?
    - A) be
    - B) bes
    - C) besi
    - D) besid

34. What is the last syllable of *study*?
    - F) y
    - G) dy
    - H) udy
    - I) tudy

35. What is the first syllable of *topic*?
    - A) t
    - B) to
    - C) top
    - D) topi

Phonics/Spelling

STOP

Name _____

Theme Test
Theme 3

Robust Vocabulary

▶ Choose the best word to complete each sentence for Numbers 36 through 45.

36. The sound of the lullaby was soft and _____.
    - (F) envious
    - (G) soothing
    - (H) chuckling
    - (I) encouraging

37. The sponge was used to _____ the water.
    - (A) absorb
    - (B) consult
    - (C) glimpse
    - (D) dissolve

38. The firefighters arrived in time to avoid a _____.
    - (F) harmony
    - (G) recommend
    - (H) catastrophe
    - (I) correspondence

39. After three days, the seeds began to _____.
    - (A) sprout
    - (B) devise
    - (C) translate
    - (D) glimpse

Robust Vocabulary

GO ON

© Harcourt • Grade 3

Name _____

Theme Test
Theme 3

40. Carlos thought hard because he wanted to make a _____ decision.

(F) luscious

(G) sensible

(H) heaving

(I) paused

41. Everyone who saw the magic show was _____.

(A) tugged

(B) swooned

(C) praised

(D) astonished

42. The rock was made of many small _____.

(F) spears

(G) strikes

(H) repairs

(I) particles

43. The coach's words were helpful and _____.

(A) rustling

(B) dodging

(C) bothersome

(D) encouraging

Robust Vocabulary

GO ON

Name _____

Theme Test
Theme 3

44. I didn't know what to do, so I asked for some _____.
    - Ⓕ din
    - Ⓖ issue
    - Ⓗ advice
    - Ⓘ rivalry

45. Is there a good book that you would _____?
    - Ⓐ roost
    - Ⓑ suppose
    - Ⓒ shudder
    - Ⓓ recommend

Robust Vocabulary

Name _____

Grammar

▶ **Read and answer Numbers 46 through 55.**

46. Which of these is a pronoun?
    - (F) it
    - (G) go
    - (H) the
    - (I) cat

47. Which of these shows the correct possessive form of *dog*?
    - (A) dogs
    - (B) dog's
    - (C) dogs'
    - (D) dogs's

48. In which of the following is the possessive noun correct?
    - (F) Martins' father is a teacher.
    - (G) The three horse's saddles were red.
    - (H) Katies brother likes to play basketball.
    - (I) The boys' coats were in the hall closet.

49. In which sentence below is the pronoun correct?
    - (A) Katie can tie his own shoe.
    - (B) The girl can skip, and she can hop.
    - (C) The car is old, but he still runs well.
    - (D) The boy liked the bike because it loved to ride.

Grammar

GO ON

Name _____

Theme Test
Theme 3

50. In which sentence below is the pronoun correct?
    - Ⓕ The teachers help the students in her class.
    - Ⓖ The boy makes their own bed each day.
    - Ⓗ Balloons are fun, but it pops easily.
    - Ⓘ The cats are cleaning their fur.

51. Which of these is a subject pronoun?
    - Ⓐ us
    - Ⓑ she
    - Ⓒ him
    - Ⓓ them

52. Which of these is an object pronoun?
    - Ⓕ he
    - Ⓖ we
    - Ⓗ her
    - Ⓘ they

53. Which sentence is written correctly?
    - Ⓐ Simon thought me had already left.
    - Ⓑ He handed me a piece of paper.
    - Ⓒ Me walked to school quickly.
    - Ⓓ She gave the ruler to I.

Grammar

GO ON

© Harcourt • Grade 3

54. Which sentence is written correctly?

　Ⓕ The boy's are waiting for the bus.

　Ⓖ The birds nest was on the ground.

　Ⓗ The dogs water dish is almost empty.

　Ⓘ The teacher's desk is always neat and clean.

55. Read the following sentence.

　　Katie proudly plays her trumpet.

　What is the antecedent of *her*?

　Ⓐ plays

　Ⓑ Katie

　Ⓒ trumpet

　Ⓓ proudly

Grammar

Name _____

Writing to a Prompt

Theme Test
Theme 3

> Suppose you had a pen pal who lived in another country. Think about what you would tell your pen pal about your life. Now write a letter telling your pen pal about your life.

Planning Page

▶ Use this space to make your notes before you begin writing. The writing on this page will NOT be scored.

Name _____

Theme Test
Theme 3

▶ **Begin writing here. The writing on this page and the next WILL be scored.**

Writing to a Prompt

Name _____

Theme Test
Theme 3

Writing to a Prompt

Name _____

Oral Reading Fluency

Theme Test
Theme 3

Carla raced up the road from the bus stop, hoping that running faster would make her warmer. Her toes were rapidly turning into icicles. In the morning, the breeze had hinted at cool weather, but her red hat, coat, and mittens had kept her warm enough. Now, however, the clouds hung dark and heavy overhead. The cool breeze had turned into an icy wind that cut right through her thick clothing and chilled her aching toes.

As Carla pulled the door closed behind her, a gust of wind blew a few snowflakes into the house. She wondered if snow would pile up on the ground during the night. "It is too early in the year for a big storm," she decided. She put away her coat, hat, and mittens. Then she hurried to thaw out with a cup of hot chocolate.

The next morning, the wind whistling around the windows woke Carla up. A thick blanket of white snow covered the ground. Carla gazed at the lacy whiteness, amazed at the change the night had brought. The snow had wrapped the world in white.

Name _____

Theme Test
Theme 3

People, plants, and animals need water to survive. Although water covers much of Earth, most of it is salt water in the oceans and seas. The water in the oceans and seas is much too salty to drink. Salt water also kills many plants that grow on Earth. The water cycle provides the fresh water that living things depend on for life.

The water cycle begins when the sun heats the water in oceans, lakes, and rivers. The heated water changes to a gas, called steam. The steam is lighter than the air so it rises into the atmosphere. High in the sky, the air is colder than the steam, so the steam cools. As it cools, it changes back into water in the form of a cloud.

The cloud grows larger and becomes heavy. When the air can no longer hold the cloud, the water changes to rain, snow, hail, or sleet, and falls to Earth. These are all forms of fresh water. On Earth, some of the water stays in the mountains or on the ground. Some goes into rivers, lakes, and oceans. Then the water cycle starts again.

Oral Reading Fluency

HARCOURT SCHOOL PUBLISHERS
STORYtown

As We Grow/Theme 3

Grade 3

Theme Tests

www.harcourtschool.com

Part No. 9997-857102-2 (Package of 12) 3-1

Breaking New Ground — Theme 4

Name _____ Date _____

Performance Summary

Student Score

READING

Reading Comprehension
    Multiple-Choice Items   _____/18
    Short-Response Open-Ended Item   _____/2
    Extended-Response Open-Ended Item   _____/4

Phonics/Spelling   _____/15

Robust Vocabulary   _____/10

    Total Student Reading Score   _____/49

LANGUAGE ARTS

    Grammar   _____/10

WRITING   _____/6

ORAL READING FLUENCY

    Passage 1   _____ Words Correct Per Minute
    Passage 2   _____ Words Correct Per Minute

(Bubble in the appropriate performance level.)

Reading

Below Basic	Basic (On-Level)	Proficient (On-Level)	Advanced
1–20	21–30	31–40	41–49
○	○	○	○

Language Arts

Below Basic	Basic (On-Level)	Proficient (On-Level)	Advanced
1–4	5–6	7–8	9–10
○	○	○	○

Writing

Below Basic	Basic (On-Level)	Proficient (On-Level)	Advanced
1–2	3–4	5	6
○	○	○	○

Oral Reading Fluency

25th Percentile	50th Percentile	75th Percentile	90th Percentile
62 WCPM	92 WCPM	120 WCPM	162 WCPM
○	○	○	○

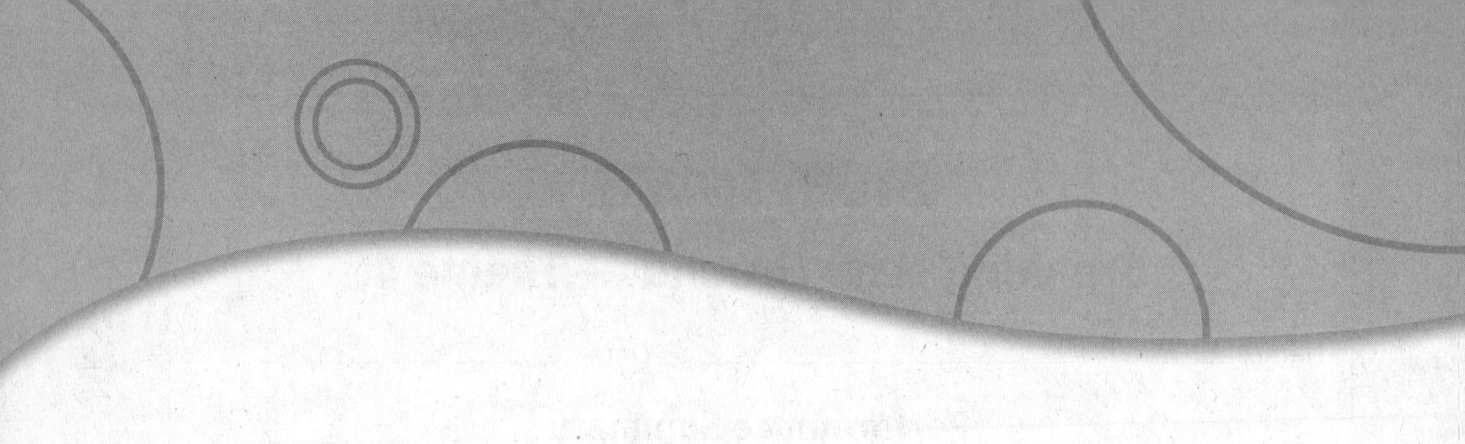

Grateful acknowledgment is made to The Cricket Magazine Group, a division of Carus Publishing Company for permission to reprint "What's For Supper?" by Julie Douglas, illustrated by Ann Strugnell from *Spider* Magazine, February 2006. Text copyright © 2006 by Julie A. Douglas; illustrations copyright © 2006 by Ann Strugnell.

Copyright © by Harcourt, Inc.

All rights reserved. No part of this publication may be reproduced or transmitted in any form or by any means, electronic or mechanical, including photocopy, recording, or any information storage and retrieval system, without permission in writing from the publisher.

Permission is hereby granted to individuals using the corresponding student's textbook or kit as the major vehicle for regular classroom instruction to photocopy entire pages from this publication in classroom quantities for instructional use and not for resale. Requests for information on other matters regarding duplication of this work should be addressed to School Permissions and Copyrights, Harcourt, Inc., 6277 Sea Harbor Drive, Orlando, Florida 32887-6777. Fax: 407-345-2418.

HARCOURT and the Harcourt Logo are trademarks of Harcourt, Inc., registered in the United States of America and/or other jurisdictions.

Printed in the United States of America

ISBN 10 0-15-368492-5
ISBN 13 978-0-15-368492-0 (Package of 12)

9 10 1409 16 15 14 13 12 11 10

If you have received these materials as examination copies free of charge, Harcourt School Publishers retains title to the materials and they may not be resold. Resale of examination copies is strictly prohibited and is illegal.

Possession of this publication in print format does not entitle users to convert this publication, or any portion of it, into electronic format.

Name _____

Reading Comprehension

Theme Test
Theme 4

▶ Read the story "The Tallest Tales" before answering Numbers 1 through 7.

The Tallest Tales

In the United States, there are special types of folktales called "tall tales." Each tall tale includes a hero. The hero can face any challenge and come out on top. Some parts of tall tales are easy to believe. Other parts are really hard to believe because they stretch the truth.

Paul Bunyan

There are tall tales about Paul Bunyan and his blue ox, Babe. They lived in camps where people cut down trees in the northern forests. Paul was so strong that he could cut down 23 trees with one swing of his axe! In one tale, Paul tied Babe to the twisting forest roads that led to the camps. Babe pulled so hard that he straightened out the roads. After Babe had finished, there were 20 miles of road left over.

Pecos Bill

Pecos Bill is a tall tale hero from Texas. He was raised by coyotes. Once, Pecos Bill caught a snake. He used it to rope a few lizards like a cowboy ropes a calf. Another time, Pecos Bill roped a big tornado. The storm kicked like a horse, but Pecos Bill stayed on. He rode the storm until it rained itself out. Pecos Bill was famous for his strength, bravery, and determination.

Reading Comprehension

GO ON

The heroes in tall tales are as brave and strong as any superhero you might read about today. Tall tale heroes were the superheroes for the children of the past. Tall tales also give us an idea about how times were long ago in America.

Write Your Own Tall Tale

1. Get a paper and pencil.
2. Choose a hero. It could be you. It could be a friend or someone you have read about. It could be someone you make up.
3. Give your hero a name.
4. Decide what your hero will do. What special skills will he or she have? How will he or she use these skills?
5. Decide where your hero will live. Will it be a city? The desert? Under the ocean?
6. Use your ideas to write a short tall tale.
7. Share your tale with a friend. Whose tale is the "tallest?"

Name _____

Theme Test
Theme 4

▶ Now answer Numbers 1 through 7. Base your answers on the passage "The Tallest Tales."

1. How are Paul Bunyan and Pecos Bill ALIKE?
   - Ⓐ Both were raised by wild animals.
   - Ⓑ Both were very strong.
   - Ⓒ Both lived in Texas.
   - Ⓓ Both had a pet ox.

2. What is one way Paul Bunyan and Pecos Bill are DIFFERENT?
   - Ⓕ Only Paul Bunyan was a hero.
   - Ⓖ Only Pecos Bill roped lizards.
   - Ⓗ Only Paul Bunyan rode a tornado.
   - Ⓘ Only Pecos Bill was a real person.

3. What is the theme of the Pecos Bill stories?
   - Ⓐ Don't trust a wild animal.
   - Ⓑ We should protect nature.
   - Ⓒ With hard work, anything is possible.
   - Ⓓ Words are more important than weapons.

4. Look at the directions for writing a tall tale. What step tells you to give your hero a name?
   - Ⓕ Step 1
   - Ⓖ Step 2
   - Ⓗ Step 3
   - Ⓘ Step 4

Reading Comprehension

3

GO ON

Name _____

Theme Test
Theme 4

5. Look at the directions for writing a tall tale. What step is the LAST step to writing a tall tale?

   Ⓐ Choose where your hero will live.

   Ⓑ Share the story with a friend.

   Ⓒ Get a paper and a pencil.

   Ⓓ Name the hero.

6. Look at the directions for writing a tall tale. Which step gives you ideas for choosing a hero?

   Ⓕ Step 1

   Ⓖ Step 2

   Ⓗ Step 3

   Ⓘ Step 4

7. Which is the BEST reference source to use to find out more about tall tales?

   Ⓐ a newspaper

   Ⓑ a thesaurus

   Ⓒ a science book

   Ⓓ an encyclopedia

Reading Comprehension

GO ON

What's For Supper?

By Julie Douglas

Art by Ann Strugnell

Everyone in Jenna's family had a job to do. Jenna's job was to set the table. Every night. It was boring.

On Monday, Jenna asked her mom, "What's for supper?"

"Fish," Mom told her.

Jenna had an idea. That night when she set the table, Jenna didn't use Mom's checkered tablecloth. Instead, she spread a clean beach towel over the table. She dragged in the lawn chairs from the garage, and she plunked down a pinkish seashell next to each plate.

"What's all this?" Mom asked when she saw it.

"We're having fish..." said Jenna, "at the beach."

Name _____

Theme Test
Theme 4

Mom smiled. The rest of Jenna's family smiled, too. After dinner, they played beachball keep-away.

The next day was Tuesday.

"I'm making mini-quiches for supper," Jenna's mom told her.

"What's a mini-quiche?" Jenna asked. Her mom opened the oven.

Rows of tiny piecrusts were lined up on a baking sheet.

"I'll fill these with eggs and vegetables and cheese," Mom said.

"Then I'll pop them back into the oven for a few minutes."

The crusts smelled delicious, but they looked so small. Jenna felt like a giant looking at an oven full of pies.

Jenna hauled her doll dishes to the kitchen and scrubbed them till they sparkled. She pulled her doll table into the living room and set it with the tiny dishes and cups. She hoped no one would break her little chairs.

"What's all this?" Mom asked when she saw it.

"We're giants," said Jenna. "People food looks very small when we eat it!"

Mom laughed. Jenna's family laughed, too.

"Fee fi fo fum," said Jenna's brother. "People food is yum, yum, yum!"

After dinner, Jenna's family stomped around and talked in big, booming giant voices.

On Wednesday, Jenna saw her mom cooking chili in the kitchen. Jenna knew just what to do. She washed some tin cans from the recycling bin till they shone like silver. On the table, Jenna folded a bandanna for each person. She set a can and a spoon at every place. In the middle of the table, Jenna put all the candles she could find.

Reading Comprehension

GO ON

"What's all this?" her mom asked.

"A campfire," said Jenna. "We're cowpokes eating beans around the fire."

Mom chuckled as she filled the cans with chili. "Cowpokes still need to wash their hands before dinner," she said.

After dinner, Jenna's family sang "Home on the Range." Grandpa played his harmonica.

On Thursday night, Jenna's mom tried a new recipe. Jenna was not sure what it was. It was green and it smelled oniony. She spread a big blanket under the table. She put the dishes and glasses on the floor. She set some rocks around the blanket. On top of the table, Jenna put a stuffed animal.

"What's all this?" Mom asked.

Jenna pointed to the goat. "He's crossing our bridge," she said.

"Our bridge?" asked Mom.

"We're trolls," Jenna explained. "We're eating something smelly and green under our bridge."

Jenna's family laughed. After a while, Jenna's mom laughed, too. Jenna was surprised: troll food was tasty. She asked for seconds.

On Friday night, Mom was making nachos for dinner. Jenna remembered eating nachos. She pushed the dining room chairs in a row. She made a circle with her jump rope in front of the chairs. She blew up balloons and decorated the dining room.

"What's all this?" her mom asked.

"We're at the circus," Jenna answered. "Remember when we ate nachos while watching the elephants last year?"

"Welcome to the Greatest Show on Earth!" Jenna called later as she helped Mom pass out the nachos.

After they finished dinner, Jenna's family took turns doing tricks in the big ring. Jenna wished she had a pet elephant.

On Saturday, Jenna's family worked in the yard. When it was dinnertime, Jenna's brother said, "I'm so hungry, I could eat a horse."

Jenna frowned. She was happy when Mom said they were going to Roberto's for pizza.

Every Sunday, Jenna's dad made a fancy dinner. He peeked into the oven and said, "Ahh, a feast fit for a king!"

Jenna pulled some crowns and princess hats from her dress-up box. She covered the table with a glittery scarf. In the middle of the table, she

Reading Comprehension

piled pennies and shiny beads. She turned on the classical music radio station. Jenna's family called each other M'lord and M'lady and bowed a lot before they sat down to eat. After dinner, her father, the king, suggested they take a royal walk around the neighborhood to look at their kingdom.

On Monday, Jenna's mom told her that she was trying another new recipe. "I've been told it's just out of this world," Mom said.

Jenna smiled. It was her job to set the table. And she had an idea!

Name _____

Theme Test
Theme 4

▶ Now answer Numbers 8 through 14. Base your answers on the story "What's For Supper?"

8. What is the theme of this story?
   Ⓕ Imagination is an important tool.
   Ⓖ Dinner is the best meal of the day.
   Ⓗ Children should always obey their parents.
   Ⓘ Families should always eat dinner together.

9. In the story, what is one thing that is the SAME about Monday and Tuesday nights?
   Ⓐ The family has fish for dinner.
   Ⓑ Jenna's mother sets the table.
   Ⓒ The family has fun at dinner.
   Ⓓ Jenna tries a new dish.

10. Where does the story take place?
    Ⓕ in a house
    Ⓖ at the circus
    Ⓗ at the beach
    Ⓘ around a campfire

11. Read the sentence from the story.

    She washed some tin cans from the recycling bin till they shone like silver.

    In the word *recycling*, what does the prefix *re-* mean?
    Ⓐ use
    Ⓑ until
    Ⓒ again
    Ⓓ before

Reading Comprehension

GO ON

Theme Test
Theme 4

12. Which of these words from the story contains a suffix?
    - F) she
    - G) food
    - H) Jenna
    - I) pinkish

13. What is the BEST reference source to use to find more stories by the same author?
    - A) an atlas
    - B) the Internet
    - C) a math book
    - D) a thesaurus

Name _____

Theme Test
Theme 4

14.  Write about how dinner at Jenna's house changes. Compare what you think dinner was like before Monday night to what it is like after. Use details and information from the story to explain your answer.

▶ Now read the article about "An Important American Artist" before answering Numbers 15 through 20.

An Important American Artist

In the 1800s, Paris was the art capital of the world. It was a beautiful city that many artists wanted to see. An American art student named Mary Cassatt went there to study.

Painting a New Way

A small group of artists in Paris had a new idea of how to paint. They painted everyday life and everyday people. This was such a new idea that some people found it shocking. These artists were known as Impressionists.

Being a Female Painter

Mary Cassatt was a very good artist. She agreed with the new ideas of the Impressionists. She began to paint the way they did. However, women at that time could not go everywhere a man could go. She could not paint all the things she wanted to paint. So, Cassatt painted people she knew. Many of them were mothers and their children. Her talent and warmth brought the scenes to life. In this way, she was still able to paint everyday people doing everyday things like the other Impressionists.

Helping Other Artists

Mary Cassatt did much to help Impressionist artists. She asked her friends and family to buy and show Impressionist paintings. This helped the painters earn money and popularity.

People today do not think Impressionist paintings are unusual. The artists who painted them are seen as some of the world's greatest painters. Mary Cassatt is an American woman who was part of that exciting time in art history.

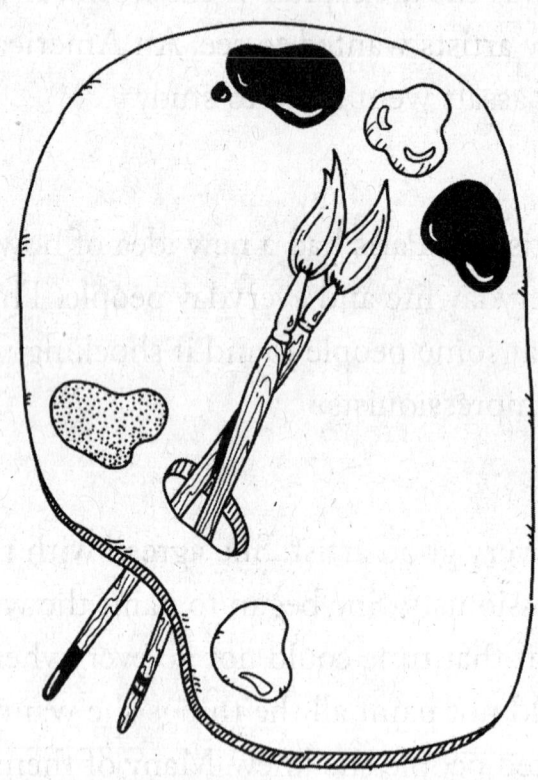

Name _____

Theme Test
Theme 4

▶ Now answer Numbers 15 through 20. Base your answers on the article "An Important American Artist."

15. What is the title of this article?
- Ⓕ "Helping Other Artists"
- Ⓖ "Painting a New Way"
- Ⓗ "Being a Female Painter"
- Ⓘ "An Important American Artist"

16. Read the sentence from the article.

    This helped the painters earn money and popularity.

    What is the suffix in the word *popularity*?
    - Ⓐ ity
    - Ⓑ pop
    - Ⓒ arity
    - Ⓓ popul

17. What is one theme of Mary Cassatt's work?
- Ⓕ Painting is an important job.
- Ⓖ Women should not be allowed to paint.
- Ⓗ Everyday people and life are important.
- Ⓘ Children should be seen and not heard.

18. What is the MAIN idea of this article?
- Ⓐ Mary Cassatt was a great painter.
- Ⓑ Mary Cassatt painted people she knew.
- Ⓒ Paris was the art capital of the world.
- Ⓓ The Impressionists formed a group in Paris.

Reading Comprehension

GO ON

Name _____

Theme Test
Theme 4

19. Which of these is an OPINION and not a fact?

   F Women should not paint.
   G Mary Cassatt painted many mothers.
   H Impressionists painted everyday life.
   I Mary Cassatt asked people to buy paintings.

20. Tell ONE way Mary Cassatt was LIKE other Impressionists. Tell ONE way Mary Cassatt was DIFFERENT from other impressionists.

_____

_____

_____

_____

_____

_____

_____

Name _____

Theme Test
Theme 4

Phonics/Spelling

▶ For Numbers 21 through 28, read each sentence that has a blank in it where a word is missing. Then fill in the circle next to the word that has the same sound as the underlined part of the model word and completes each sentence.

21. o<u>ur</u>

   Sally is in the _____ grade.

   Ⓐ flour
   Ⓑ sore
   Ⓒ third
   Ⓓ fourth

22. <u>oar</u>

   The fans kept their eyes on the _____.

   Ⓕ field
   Ⓖ roar
   Ⓗ players
   Ⓘ scoreboard

23. m<u>ore</u>

   I love to visit the _____.

   Ⓐ soar
   Ⓑ park
   Ⓒ forest
   Ⓓ office

Phonics/Spelling

GO ON

Name _____

Theme Test
Theme 4

24. swarm

   I hope the weather will be _____.

   (F) hot
   (G) warm
   (H) farm
   (I) breezy

25. purr

   The cat was behind the _____.

   (A) box
   (B) cure
   (C) pillow
   (D) curtain

26. first

   After the long day, I was very _____.

   (F) tired
   (G) board
   (H) thirsty
   (I) hungry

27. nurse

   I was surprised that I knew the whole _____ by heart.

   (A) source
   (B) poem
   (C) verse
   (D) puddle

Phonics/Spelling

GO ON

Name _____

Theme Test
Theme 4

28. clerk

Rita raised her hand to _____ the teacher's question.

Ⓕ answer

Ⓖ ask

Ⓗ perfect

Ⓘ tell

▶ **For Numbers 29 through 35, read each sentence that has a blank in it where a word is missing. Choose the correct form of the word to complete the sentence.**

29. He walked _____ down the hall.

Ⓐ quiet

Ⓑ quieter

Ⓒ quietly

Ⓓ quietest

30. Who has the _____ bike?

Ⓕ fastful

Ⓖ fastly

Ⓗ fasting

Ⓘ fastest

31. I am very _____ for my family.

Ⓐ thankly

Ⓑ thanking

Ⓒ thankful

Ⓓ thank

Phonics/Spelling   19   GO ON

Name _____

Theme Test
Theme 4

32. An hour is _____ than a minute.
    - Ⓕ long
    - Ⓖ longer
    - Ⓗ longest
    - Ⓘ longing

33. To check your work after you read, _____ the lesson.
    - Ⓐ read
    - Ⓑ reread
    - Ⓒ unread
    - Ⓓ disread

34. He wasn't nice, so I began to _____ him.
    - Ⓕ like
    - Ⓖ relike
    - Ⓗ unlike
    - Ⓘ dislike

35. There was a treasure under the sand, and I wanted to _____ it.
    - Ⓐ cover
    - Ⓑ recover
    - Ⓒ uncover
    - Ⓓ covering

Phonics/Spelling

Name _____

Robust Vocabulary

Theme Test
Theme 4

▶ **Choose the best word to complete each sentence for Numbers 36 through 45.**

36. The mother's touch was gentle and _____.
    - (F) brittle
    - (G) tender
    - (H) disguised
    - (I) ingenious

37. Michael's good manners are very _____.
    - (A) vain
    - (B) swift
    - (C) drowsy
    - (D) charming

38. Laura didn't want to be heard, so she _____ quietly into the room.
    - (F) crept
    - (G) yanked
    - (H) suggested
    - (I) exclaimed

39. You have to be pretty smart to _____ Sadie.
    - (A) outwit
    - (B) devise
    - (C) translate
    - (D) recommend

Robust Vocabulary

GO ON

Name _____

Theme Test
Theme 4

40. I spilled milk on my picture, and now it is _____.

Ⓕ ruined

Ⓖ glorious

Ⓗ flawless

Ⓘ enormous

41. I am grateful for the _____ I have with my good friend.

Ⓐ racket

Ⓑ streak

Ⓒ dilemma

Ⓓ camaraderie

42. After being away for days, I was _____ to be home.

Ⓕ delighted

Ⓖ composed

Ⓗ rehearsed

Ⓘ overheard

43. The teacher was _____ the noisy children.

Ⓐ scolding

Ⓑ glancing

Ⓒ charging

Ⓓ chuckling

44. When they met again, the two old friends _____.

Ⓕ criticized

Ⓖ praised

Ⓗ embraced

Ⓘ disguised

Robust Vocabulary

22

GO ON

Name _____

45. This beautiful painting is definitely a _____.
- Ⓐ burden
- Ⓑ heritage
- Ⓒ dialogue
- Ⓓ masterpiece

Robust Vocabulary

Name _____

Theme Test
Theme 4

Grammar

▶ **Read and answer Numbers 46 through 55.**

46. Which sentence is written correctly?
    - F This is candy sweet.
    - G Here orange is the cat.
    - H I jumped on big the bed.
    - I I really liked the colorful fish.

47. This is the _____ cake I've ever seen.
    - A big
    - B bigs
    - C bigger
    - D biggest

48. Which sentence is written correctly?
    - F Beth has the most carrots.
    - G Please give me most peas.
    - H Rhonda likes most peas than carrots.
    - I Aaron has most peas than anyone else.

49. Her book is _____ than mine.
    - A long
    - B longs
    - C longer
    - D longest

Grammar   24   GO ON

50. Which of these is an article?
   - Ⓕ it
   - Ⓖ an
   - Ⓗ go
   - Ⓘ will

51. Which of these is a verb?
   - Ⓐ cat
   - Ⓑ run
   - Ⓒ more
   - Ⓓ yellow

52. Which sentence is written correctly?
   - Ⓕ She jump.
   - Ⓖ I walks slowly.
   - Ⓗ He run to the store.
   - Ⓘ They swim very quickly.

53. Which sentence is written correctly?
   - Ⓐ He has a stickers.
   - Ⓑ She brought the flowers.
   - Ⓒ Mary ate a French fries.
   - Ⓓ William wore an blue shoes.

54. Which of these is an adjective?
   - Ⓕ Paul
   - Ⓖ bird
   - Ⓗ jump
   - Ⓘ pretty

Grammar

Name _____

Theme Test
Theme 4

55. The hen laid _____ egg.
    Ⓐ a
    Ⓑ an
    Ⓒ it
    Ⓓ three

Grammar

Name _____

Writing to a Prompt

Theme Test
Theme 4

> When we use our imagination, we can go anywhere.
> Think about taking a trip to another planet.
> Now write a story about taking a trip to another planet.

Planning Page

▶ Use this space to make your notes before you begin writing.
The writing on this page will NOT be scored.

_____
_____
_____
_____
_____
_____
_____
_____
_____

GO ON

Name _____

Theme Test
Theme 4

▶ **Begin writing here. The writing on this page and the next WILL be scored.**

Writing to a Prompt

28

GO ON

© Harcourt • Grade 3

Name _____

Name _____

Oral Reading Fluency

Theme Test
Theme 4

John woke up before sunrise, got dressed, and ate breakfast. Then he searched for his baseball glove. In a few minutes, his uncle would arrive to take him to his first major league baseball game. John had loved baseball for as long as he could remember.

When his uncle drove up, John scrambled into the car. After a three-hour drive, John felt excitement rush through him as they arrived at the huge parking lot near the baseball park.

John and his uncle located their seats and sat down. The umpire yelled, "Play ball!" and the game began. About halfway through the game, a player hit a ball that appeared to curve directly toward John. He quickly lifted his hand in its baseball glove as high above his head as he could. All of a sudden, he felt his arm bending back, and he almost fell over. He had caught the ball!

The rest of the game passed in a blur for John. That night, he fell asleep dreaming about playing catcher in his first big league baseball game!

Before Europeans arrived in North America, the Sioux Indian tribe lived on the American plains for hundreds of years. The people of the Sioux tribe have always had many stories to tell about their long history.

Long ago, the Sioux told their stories with pictures instead of words. The pictures were painted on the skins of animals that the tribe had hunted. Sioux artists used pictures to tell about events that had happened to the tribe.

The Sioux measured a year from one winter to the next, so these picture stories became known as "winter counts." Each picture on the winter count told about one year. As time passed, more and more pictures were added to the winter count. A winter count might tell the stories of wars or big hunts. Later, Sioux winter counts told stories about meeting Europeans. Winter counts help us understand what life was like for the Sioux people many years ago.

Could you make a winter count to tell the story of your life? What would it look like? What kinds of stories do you have to tell?

HARCOURT SCHOOL PUBLISHERS
STORYtown

Tales to Tell/Theme 4

Grade 3

Theme Tests

www.harcourtschool.com

ISBN-13: 978-0-15-368492-0
ISBN-10: 0-15-368492-5

Part No. 9997-87103-0   (Package of 12)

Breaking New Ground — Theme 5

Name _____ Date _____

Performance Summary

Student Score

READING

Reading Comprehension
- Multiple-Choice Items _____/18
- Short-Response Open-Ended Item _____/2
- Extended-Response Open-Ended Item _____/4

Phonics/Spelling _____/15

Robust Vocabulary _____/10

Total Student Reading Score _____/49

LANGUAGE ARTS

Grammar _____/10

WRITING _____/6

ORAL READING FLUENCY

Passage 1 _____ Words Correct Per Minute
Passage 2 _____ Words Correct Per Minute

(Bubble in the appropriate performance level.)

Reading

Below Basic	Basic (On-Level)	Proficient (On-Level)	Advanced
1–20	21–30	31–40	41–49
○	○	○	○

Language Arts

Below Basic	Basic (On-Level)	Proficient (On-Level)	Advanced
1–4	5–6	7–8	9–10
○	○	○	○

Writing

Below Basic	Basic (On-Level)	Proficient (On-Level)	Advanced
1–2	3–4	5	6
○	○	○	○

Oral Reading Fluency

25th Percentile	50th Percentile	75th Percentile	90th Percentile
78 WCPM	107 WCPM	137 WCPM	162 WCPM
○	○	○	○

Grateful acknowledgment is made to The Cricket Magazine Group, a division of Carus Publishing Company for permission to reprint "The Hoot and Holler Hat Dance: A Folktale from Ghana" by Laura S. Sassi, illustrated by Jennifer Hewitson from *Spider* Magazine, November 2004. Copyright © 2004 by Carus Publishing Company.

Copyright © by Harcourt, Inc.

All rights reserved. No part of this publication may be reproduced or transmitted in any form or by any means, electronic or mechanical, including photocopy, recording, or any information storage and retrieval system, without permission in writing from the publisher.

Permission is hereby granted to individuals using the corresponding student's textbook or kit as the major vehicle for regular classroom instruction to photocopy entire pages from this publication in classroom quantities for instructional use and not for resale. Requests for information on other matters regarding duplication of this work should be addressed to School Permissions and Copyrights, Harcourt, Inc., 6277 Sea Harbor Drive, Orlando, Florida 32887-6777. Fax: 407-345-2418.

HARCOURT and the Harcourt Logo are trademarks of Harcourt, Inc., registered in the United States of America and/or other jurisdictions.

Printed in the United States of America

ISBN 10 0-15-368492-5
ISBN 13 978-0-15-368492-0 (Package of 12)

9 10 1409 16 15 14 13 12 11 10

If you have received these materials as examination copies free of charge, Harcourt School Publishers retains title to the materials and they may not be resold. Resale of examination copies is strictly prohibited and is illegal.

Possession of this publication in print format does not entitle users to convert this publication, or any portion of it, into electronic format.

Reading Comprehension

Theme Test · Theme 5

▶ Read the story "Teamwork in the Herd" before answering Numbers 1 through 7.

Teamwork in the Herd

Elephant Herds

Imagine that you saw a group of elephants in the wild. You would see about 11 adults and two or three young elephants. However, there is something very interesting about each of these herds. All the adult elephants in the herd are female. Males live separately when they reach about 14 years of age.

Leader of the Herd

Each herd has a leader, the oldest female elephant. She makes all the important decisions for the herd. She decides whether the herd should fight if it is attacked. She also teaches what she has learned to the younger group of elephants. Since the lifetime of an elephant can be as long as 60 years, an older elephant really knows a lot.

Babies in the Herd

    Each of the calves, or babies, is precious. Each one is treated with kindness and love. Calves drink only milk, while older elephants eat only plants. The mother must eat a lot of greens or vegetation to produce enough milk. The solution? Each mother selects other elephants to "babysit" for her calf. The babysitter protects the calf, teaches it, and plays with it. Meanwhile, the mother elephant can take care of getting the nutrition she needs to keep herself and her baby healthy. That's teamwork!

Name _____

Theme Test
Theme 5

▶ Now answer Numbers 1 through 7. Base your answers on the article "Teamwork in the Herd."

1. Why does a mother elephant need a babysitter for her calf?
   Ⓐ She has to make decisions for the herd.
   Ⓑ She needs to be able to find food.
   Ⓒ She cannot produce enough milk herself.
   Ⓓ She knows she will not be able to care for it.

2. According to the article, what must happen BEFORE an elephant can become the leader of the herd?
   Ⓕ She must give birth.
   Ⓖ She must find a babysitter
   Ⓗ She must be at least 14 years old.
   Ⓘ She must be the oldest elephant in the herd.

3. Which of these is the BEST reference source to use to learn more about elephants?
   Ⓐ an almanac
   Ⓑ a science magazine
   Ⓒ a dictionary
   Ⓓ an atlas

4. What does the author MOST want the reader to understand?
   Ⓕ Elephants fight when the herd is in danger.
   Ⓖ Elephant herds work as a team.
   Ⓗ Baby elephants drink only milk.
   Ⓘ Elephants eat a lot of food.

Reading Comprehension   3   GO ON

Name _____

Theme Test
Theme 5

5. Read the sentence from the article.

   Each of the calves, or babies, is precious.

   Which word means almost the SAME as *precious*?

   Ⓐ big
   Ⓑ smart
   Ⓒ hungry
   Ⓓ valuable

6. Read the sentence from the article.

   She decides whether the herd should fight if it is attacked.

   Which of the following is a homophone of *whether*?

   Ⓕ if
   Ⓖ until
   Ⓗ attacked
   Ⓘ weather

Reading Comprehension

GO ON

Name _____

Theme Test

Theme 5

7. The article explains that each elephant in a herd plays an important role. Choose ONE of these roles, and explain what effect this role has on the herd.

_____

_____

_____

_____

_____

_____

Reading Comprehension

GO ON

Read the story "The Skateboard Solution" before answering Numbers 8 through 13.

The Skateboard Solution

James wanted a skateboard, but his parents had made it clear that they weren't going to buy one for him right now. They had told James time after time that he had to find a different way to get one.

That was disappointing. James sat on his bed and stared at his other stuff. He looked at all the items he didn't use anymore, thinking that he just wanted one thing: a skateboard. James sat up quickly. He had just thought of something. Even though he didn't play with some of his things anymore, maybe someone else would. James started putting all of the things he didn't use anymore into a huge pile.

James's mother came in and asked what he was doing.

"I'm planning a yard sale to earn money for a skateboard," said James.

James's mother said, "I have a suggestion. My friend, Anna Lopez, recycles toys. She collects old toys to give to kids who need them. In return, maybe she can find a skateboard for you. You might want to take your things to her and see if she has a skateboard to trade."

They drove to Anna's house. James dropped off the toys, and Anna seemed pleased with each one. She told him that she knew that there were several children in the community who would be happy to have the items James brought in. "I'd like to look for a skateboard, please," he asked.

"Go right ahead," Anna told him. She pointed to the room in her basement where she stored all the used toys she had received.

James was happy that he had given his toys where they would do some good. He started to look through the used toys. After rummaging for over fifteen minutes, James was disappointed and discouraged. He didn't find a skateboard among Anna's other toys.

"I'll write down your name and telephone number," Anna offered. "If someone drops off a skateboard, I'll call you, and you can have it."

The next day, James found a message on the table from his mother. It read, "Anna has a 'wheely' great surprise for you."

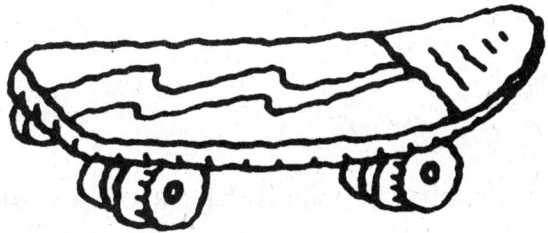

Name _____

Theme Test
Theme 5

▶ **Now answer Numbers 8 through 13. Base your answers on the story "The Skateboard Solution."**

8. Read the sentence from the story.

    It read, "Anna has a 'wheely' great surprise for you."

    What is the *"wheely" great surprise* in this sentence?

    Ⓐ a hat
    Ⓑ a telephone
    Ⓒ a new friend
    Ⓓ a skateboard

9. Which of the following words BEST describes James?

    Ⓕ lazy
    Ⓖ angry
    Ⓗ grumpy
    Ⓘ determined

10. What event happens FIRST?

    Ⓐ James plans a yard sale.
    Ⓑ James takes toys to Anna's house.
    Ⓒ James finds a message from his mother.
    Ⓓ Anna writes down James's phone number.

11. What does the author MOST want the reader to understand?

    Ⓕ Skateboards are cool toys.
    Ⓖ Recycling is a good solution for everyone.
    Ⓗ Yard sales don't usually work out very well.
    Ⓘ Parents don't always understand their children.

Reading Comprehension

GO ON

Name _____

Theme Test
Theme 5

12. Why does James become discouraged while he is at Anna's house?
    - Ⓐ She will not buy him a skateboard.
    - Ⓑ She does not have what he wanted.
    - Ⓒ She has a messy house.
    - Ⓓ She isn't very nice.

Name _____

Theme Test
Theme 5

13. Explain how the story shows that good things come from helping others. Use details and information from the story to explain your answer.

_____
_____
_____
_____
_____
_____
_____
_____
_____

Reading Comprehension

10

GO ON

© Harcourt • Grade 3

The Hoot and Holler Hat Dance

A Folk Tale from Ghana
Retold by Laura S. Sassi
Art by Jennifer Hewitson

Anansi, the Spider, was once very handsome, with eight long legs, a round little belly, and a stunning head of hair. He was also very greedy and hoarded everything in sight. Alas, his never-ending appetite eventually cost him his hair.

It happened at harvest time. "Make yourself useful, dear, and go help your mama pick the corn," Anansi's wife said to him one morning as he lounged lazily in his web.

"Ugh," Anansi groaned, for the mere mention of work made his tummy growl. Nevertheless, he grabbed his hat and started slowly on his way.

Name _____

Theme Test
Theme 5

To his dismay, the path was hot and dusty, and tasty tidbits were few and far between. Only the thought of Mama's delicious bean stew kept him going.

By the time he arrived, all he could think about was spicy beans simmering in Mama's famous stew. "I want to eat!" he hollered as he pushed open the gate.

"Not till you finish picking the corn!" Mama exclaimed. Then, handing him a basket to fill, she scurried back to the kitchen.

Soon, the field was filled with the aroma of Mama's beans and onions. To his credit, Anansi tried to ignore the smell. First he turned this way, then he turned that. Still, the wonderful fragrance swirled all around him. "I must eat!" he panted, putting down his basket.

Just then, Mama crossed the field with a calabash bowl.

"Stew at last!" he rejoiced, as he gulped his first mouthful. Then he spat, for it was only water!

"We'll feast when you finish," Mama scolded.

But Anansi could bear it no longer. When Mama disappeared, he dashed to the kitchen. The bean stew hissed and bubbled in the pot. "Mmm!" Anansi cried. In seconds he was greedily guzzling spoonful after spoonful.

But little spoonfuls were not enough. "I want more!" he said. Yanking off his hat and turning it upside down, he filled it to the brim.

Just then he spotted Okra, the cat. "Uh-oh!" Anansi yelped, quickly plopping his bean-filled hat on his head. Then he smiled his handsomest smile.

"Greetings, Anansi," Okra purred politely. "What are you doing here?"

Reading Comprehension   12   GO ON

"Just helping dear old Mama with the harvest," Anansi replied with syrupy sweetness.

But he didn't feel sweet. He felt hot, so hot it hurt! He shook his hat a little, but the boiling beans still burned. He shook his hat a little faster, but the stew still scalded. He jumped. He danced. He jiggled his hat. Still, the beans burned hotter and hotter.

Sensing a commotion, Kraman, the dog, appeared. "What is wrong with you?" he woofed.

"Nothing!" Anansi hollered. "Don't you know? It's Hat-Shaking Day!"

"Never heard of it," Kraman barked.

"Why, yes!" Anansi shouted, shaking his head faster and faster.

"It happens once a year! Hat-Shaking Day! Ha—Ha—Hat-Shaking Day!" Anansi sang, hooting and hollering down the path. Finally, he could stand it no longer. With one final howl, he ripped off his hat.

Okra and Kraman roared with laughter as beans and onions spilled everywhere. Soon the birds and bugs joined in, for greedy Anansi was quite a sight. The beans had completely burned off his hair, leaving him as bald as a corn kernel!

Alas, his hair never grew back. That is why to this day, Anansi shuffles in shame through the grass, where no one can see his big, bald head.

Name _____

Theme Test

Theme 5

▶ Now answer Numbers 14 through 20. Base your answers on the story "The Hoot and Holler Hat Dance."

14. Which set of words from the story are homophones?
    - Ⓕ to/too
    - Ⓖ hat/hot
    - Ⓗ alas/grass
    - Ⓘ jumped/jiggled

15. Where did this story come from originally?
    - Ⓐ India
    - Ⓑ Spain
    - Ⓒ Ghana
    - Ⓓ North America

16. Why does Anansi put the hat on his head?
    - Ⓕ His head is cold.
    - Ⓖ It is Hat Shaking Day.
    - Ⓗ He wants to surprise his mother.
    - Ⓘ He does not want the cat to see him eating.

17. Which of the following happens AFTER Anansi puts the hat on his head?
    - Ⓐ Kraman laughs.
    - Ⓑ He sees Okra, the cat.
    - Ⓒ He wants to eat some stew.
    - Ⓓ His mother brings him some water.

Reading Comprehension

14

GO ON

© Harcourt • Grade 3

18. What does the author MOST want the reader to understand?

   F Bean stew is very hot.

   G Anansi is bald to this day.

   H It does not pay to be dishonest.

   I Cats do not make good friends.

19. Which of these words is a homophone of the word *so*?

   A no

   B grow

   C sew

   D soup

20. What was Anansi supposed to be doing when he ate the stew?

   F hunting

   G sleeping

   H picking corn

   I feeding the cat

Name _____

Phonics/Spelling

▶ For Numbers 21 through 28, read each sentence that has a blank in it where a word is missing. Choose the word that has the same sound as the underlined part of the model word and that also completes the sentence.

Theme Test
Theme 5

21. cr<u>u</u>ise

   Sally _____ the ball.

   Ⓐ new
   Ⓑ caught
   Ⓒ threw
   Ⓓ hit

22. t<u>oo</u>k

   I needed a new _____ for my coat rack.

   Ⓕ tool
   Ⓖ hook
   Ⓗ mule
   Ⓘ balloon

23. n<u>ew</u>s

   I wanted to see the funny _____.

   Ⓐ blew
   Ⓑ door
   Ⓒ book
   Ⓓ cartoon

Phonics/Spelling

GO ON

Name _____

Theme Test
Theme 5

24. cool

   I hope to visit the _____ one day.

   Ⓕ brook

   Ⓖ dome

   Ⓗ pool

   Ⓘ park

25. ought

   I couldn't believe that he _____ that fish.

   Ⓐ thought

   Ⓑ tipped

   Ⓒ caught

   Ⓓ swallowed

26. thaw

   I needed to use a _____.

   Ⓕ pan

   Ⓖ straw

   Ⓗ spoon

   Ⓘ lawn

27. almost

   The answer was _____.

   Ⓐ yes

   Ⓑ false

   Ⓒ easy

   Ⓓ caught

Phonics/Spelling

GO ON

Name _____

Theme Test
Theme 5

28. long

He _____ his homework.

Ⓕ did
Ⓖ lost
Ⓗ almost
Ⓘ misplaced

Phonics/Spelling   18   GO ON

Name _____

Theme Test
Theme 5

▶ **For Numbers 29 through 35, read the sentence that has a blank in it where a word is missing. Choose the correct form of the word to complete the sentence.**

29. She was angry because he _____ her computer.
- (A) reused
- (B) misused
- (C) preused
- (D) inused

30. Don't forget to _____ the oven.
- (F) unheat
- (G) misheat
- (H) preheat
- (I) inheat

31. I need to _____ the data into the computer.
- (A) reput
- (B) misput
- (C) unput
- (D) input

32. What syllable in the word medium makes the /ə/ sound?
- (F) me
- (G) di
- (H) um
- (I) medi

Phonics/Spelling

19

GO ON

Name _____

Theme Test
Theme 5

33. What syllable in the word alone makes the /ə/ sound?

   A) a
   B) lon
   C) alo
   D) lone

34. What syllable in the word easily makes the /ə/ sound?

   F) e
   G) as
   H) i
   I) ly

35. What syllable in the word gallop makes the /ə/ sound?

   A) gal
   B) ll
   C) al
   D) op

Phonics/Spelling

Name _____

Robust Vocabulary

Theme Test
Theme 5

▶ **Choose the best word to complete each sentence for Numbers 36 through 45.**

36. Because the group had very little water, they _____ it carefully.
    - (F) inverted
    - (G) blanketed
    - (H) conserved
    - (I) transferred

37. When Paolo was asked to speak, he became nervous and _____.
    - (A) realistic
    - (B) flustered
    - (C) functional
    - (D) affordable

38. We were not allowed to work in groups, so we had to work _____.
    - (F) eagerly
    - (G) deliberately
    - (H) permanently
    - (I) individually

39. It was hard to see because the lights were so _____.
    - (A) dim
    - (B) strict
    - (C) absence
    - (D) decent

Robust Vocabulary

21

GO ON

© Harcourt • Grade 3

Name _____

Theme Test
Theme 5

40. The model spaceships were very _____.

    F shifting
    G required
    H fluttering
    I futuristic

41. When the bird sees a fish, it _____ down from above.

    A swoops
    B shelters
    C drifts
    D dozes

42. In the desert, water is very _____.

    F bleak
    G scarce
    H visible
    I contented

43. The crazy story was completely _____.

    A ample
    B effective
    C nocturnal
    D ridiculous

44. I couldn't see the floor through all of the _____.

    F effort
    G clutter
    H presentation
    I responsibility

Robust Vocabulary

GO ON

Name _____

45. He wanted to talk, so he _____ to me.
Ⓐ confused
Ⓑ beckoned
Ⓒ mentioned
Ⓓ collaborated

Robust Vocabulary

Name _____

Grammar

Theme Test
Theme 5

▶ Read and answer Numbers 46 through 55.

46. Which sentence is written correctly?

   Ⓕ I be here.
   Ⓖ He is walking.
   Ⓗ They be having a party.
   Ⓘ Is you going to be home this afternoon?

47. Which of these is a helping verb?

   Ⓐ run
   Ⓑ jump
   Ⓒ could
   Ⓓ bring

48. What is the main verb in this sentence?

   You should not have gone to the store alone.

   Ⓕ have
   Ⓖ gone
   Ⓗ alone
   Ⓘ should

49. Which of these verbs is in the present-tense?

   Ⓐ go
   Ⓑ had
   Ⓒ ran
   Ⓓ will catch

Grammar
24
GO ON

Name _____

Theme Test
Theme 5

50. Which of these verbs is in the past-tense?
    - F) jump
    - G) yell
    - H) walked
    - I) will ride

51. Which of these verbs is in the future-tense?
    - A) hold
    - B) had marched
    - C) smiles
    - D) will drive

52. Which word in this sentence is a helping verb?

    They will be late for school.

    - F) be
    - G) for
    - H) will
    - I) school

53. Which sentence is written correctly?
    - A) Will she play in the game tomorrow?
    - B) He will ran in the big race.
    - C) He jump high yesterday.
    - D) She will wins.

Grammar

GO ON

54. Which sentence is written correctly?

    F) I is going swimming.

    G) They are floating.

    H) He be rolling.

    I) She am fast.

55. Which sentence is written correctly in the present-tense?

    A) He goes to the store.

    B) Rita fly a kite after class.

    C) Martha read a good book.

    D) She bring flowers to the teacher.

Name _____

Theme Test
Theme 5

Writing to a Prompt

> Most people have been part of a team.
> Think about a time when you were part of a team.
> Now explain what you did to help the team.

Planning Page

▶ Use this space to make your notes before you begin writing. The writing on this page will NOT be scored.

_____
_____
_____
_____
_____
_____
_____
_____
_____
_____

Name _____

**Theme Test
Theme 5**

▶ **Begin writing here. The writing on this page and the next WILL be scored.**

Writing to a Prompt

Name _____

Theme Test
Theme 5

_____

_____

_____

_____

_____

_____

_____

_____

_____

_____

_____

_____

_____

_____

_____

Writing to a Prompt

Name _____

Oral Reading Fluency

Theme Test
Theme 5

    I live on the third floor of a five-story apartment building with my mom, dad, and little sister Clara.

    Many friendly people live in our building. Mrs. Morton lives next door with her prize-winning poodle. Sometimes we pass them in the elevator or on the sidewalk. Dad says the dog keeps Mrs. Morton company. I'd like to have a dog, too, but mom says dogs are too much work. Besides, she says, I have Clara to keep me company.

    When I'm not with Clara, I'm with my best friend Lin. She lives on the first floor. Lin's family is from China. Each morning, I leave my apartment and ride the elevator to the first floor where Lin waits for me. We walk to the bus stop, chatting and giggling. Sometimes after school, Lin and I sit at the big table in her living room and finish our homework. On Saturdays, we like to play board games. I know how lucky I am to have a friend in the building!

    My mom and dad have friends in the building, too. Mr. and Mrs. Sanchez live upstairs. Sometimes they come downstairs and play cards with my parents. Clara and I can hear them laughing even after we go to bed.

    We all laugh a lot in our building full of friends.

Oral Reading Fluency

Name _____

Theme Test
Theme 5

When you visit a park, do you see broken bottles on the ground or dirty plastic bags? Do you notice empty candy boxes and crushed cans when you look down at the sidewalk? If you do, you understand how garbage can spoil the neighborhoods we live in, if it isn't picked up and thrown away.

Garbage can be dangerous, if it is not in the right place. If there is broken glass on the ground at a park, someone could get cut by the glass while playing. Garbage is not safe for nature. Plastic bottles on grass will keep it from growing. Animals such as birds, squirrels, and rabbits can become tangled in plastic strings so that they can't move. They might be injured or die.

Each person who lives in a neighborhood should keep the neighborhood clean. If everyone picked up one piece of garbage each day, just imagine how much cleaner our neighborhoods would be. You can make a difference. The next time you see a piece of trash on the ground, pick it up and help make your neighborhood a nicer place.

Oral Reading Fluency

HARCOURT SCHOOL PUBLISHERS
STORYtown

A Place for All/Theme 5

Grade 3

Theme Tests

www.harcourtschool.com

ISBN-13: 978-0-15-368492-0
ISBN-10: 0-15-368492-5

Breaking New Ground — Theme 6

Name _____ Date _____

Performance Summary

Student Score

READING

Reading Comprehension
- Multiple-Choice Items _____/18
- Short-Response Open-Ended Item _____/2
- Extended-Response Open-Ended Item _____/4

Phonics/Spelling _____/15

Robust Vocabulary _____/10

Total Student Reading Score _____/49

LANGUAGE ARTS
- Grammar _____/10

WRITING _____/6

ORAL READING FLUENCY
- Passage 1 _____ Words Correct Per Minute
- Passage 2 _____ Words Correct Per Minute

(Bubble in the appropriate performance level.)

Reading

Below Basic	Basic (On-Level)	Proficient (On-Level)	Advanced
1–20	21–30	31–40	41–49
○	○	○	○

Language Arts

Below Basic	Basic (On-Level)	Proficient (On-Level)	Advanced
1–4	5–6	7–8	9–10
○	○	○	○

Writing

Below Basic	Basic (On-Level)	Proficient (On-Level)	Advanced
1–2	3–4	5	6
○	○	○	○

Oral Reading Fluency

25th Percentile	50th Percentile	75th Percentile	90th Percentile
78 WCPM	107 WCPM	137 WCPM	162 WCPM
○	○	○	○

Grateful acknowledgment is made to Candlewick Press, Inc., Cambridge, MA, on behalf of Walker Books Ltd., London, for permission to reprint *Bringing Down the Moon* by Jonathan Emmett, illustrated by Vanessa Cabban. Text copyright © 2001 by Jonathan Emmett; illustrations copyright © 2001 by Vanessa Cabban.

Copyright © by Harcourt, Inc.

All rights reserved. No part of this publication may be reproduced or transmitted in any form or by any means, electronic or mechanical, including photocopy, recording, or any information storage and retrieval system, without permission in writing from the publisher.

Permission is hereby granted to individuals using the corresponding student's textbook or kit as the major vehicle for regular classroom instruction to photocopy entire pages from this publication in classroom quantities for instructional use and not for resale. Requests for information on other matters regarding duplication of this work should be addressed to School Permissions and Copyrights, Harcourt, Inc., 6277 Sea Harbor Drive, Orlando, Florida 32887-6777. Fax: 407-345-2418.

HARCOURT and the Harcourt Logo are trademarks of Harcourt, Inc., registered in the United States of America and/or other jurisdictions.

Printed in the United States of America

ISBN 10 0-15-368492-5
ISBN 13 978-0-15-368492-0 (Package of 12)

9 10 1409 16 15 14 13 12 11 10

If you have received these materials as examination copies free of charge, Harcourt School Publishers retains title to the materials and they may not be resold. Resale of examination copies is strictly prohibited and is illegal.

Possession of this publication in print format does not entitle users to convert this publication, or any portion of it, into electronic format.

Name _____

Reading Comprehension

▶ Read the article "Earth's Tiniest Creatures" before answering Numbers 1 through 7.

Earth's Tiniest Creatures

What are plankton?

Plankton are tiny creatures that live in the world's oceans and lakes. Some are so tiny that you cannot see them with your eyes. They are very small. They are also very important.

How do they move?

Plankton do not move on their own. They are too small and too weak. They move through the oceans on currents. In fact, their name comes from a Greek word, *planktos*, which means "drifting."

What kinds are there?

There are two main types of plankton. One is plant plankton, and the other is animal plankton. Plant plankton have only one cell and are the tiniest creatures in the ocean. Animal plankton are larger with many cells. They are easier to see.

Why are they important?

Plankton are important to Earth's ocean life. One reason is that plant plankton produces oxygen, just as green plants do on land. The fish in the water need oxygen to breathe, just as people do. Fish take the oxygen from the water with their gills.

Another reason these tiny creatures are important is that they are the most basic food in the oceans. All of the ocean animals depend on them in some way. For example, the plants are eaten by animal plankton. Then larger animals eat them. If there were no plankton in the oceans, the food web would not be complete.

It's amazing to think about how something so small can be so big! Plankton play an important role in our world.

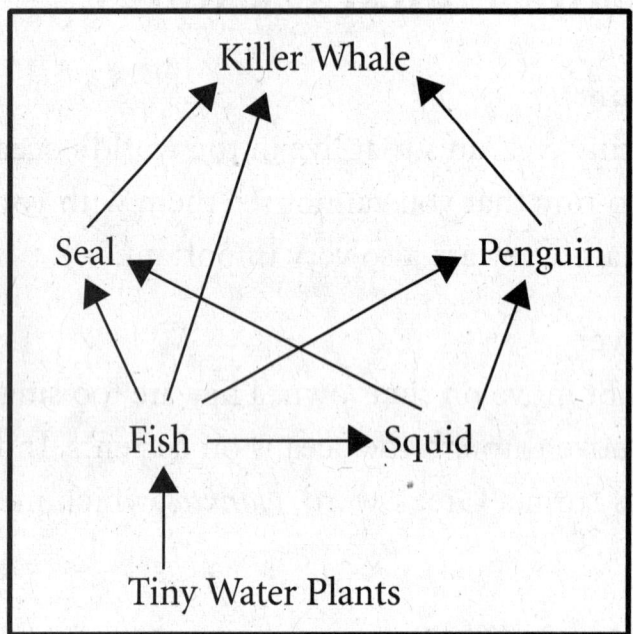

Name _____

Theme Test
Theme 6

▶ Now answer Numbers 1 through 7. Base your answers on the article "Earth's Tiniest Creatures."

1. Why does the author say that plankton are "big" even though they are small in size?
   Ⓐ Plankton can drift on currents.
   Ⓑ Some can be seen without a microscope.
   Ⓒ Plankton are important to Earth's ocean life.
   Ⓓ Animal plankton are bigger than plant plankton.

2. What would happen if there were fewer plankton in the ocean?
   Ⓕ The ocean would dry up.
   Ⓖ More plants would grow.
   Ⓗ Fewer animals could live there.
   Ⓘ The remaining plankton would grow bigger.

3. Read the sentence from the article.

   They move through the oceans on currents.

   What does the word *currents* mean in this sentence?
   Ⓐ up to date
   Ⓑ moving water
   Ⓒ a kind of plankton
   Ⓓ a group of sea animals

4. What is the MAIN idea of this article?
   Ⓕ Plankton are small.
   Ⓖ Plankton are important.
   Ⓗ Plankton live in bodies of water.
   Ⓘ Plankton are too weak to move on their own.

Reading Comprehension

3

GO ON

Name _____

Theme Test
Theme 6

5. What is the MAIN difference between plant and animal plankton?

   Ⓐ Plant plankton are smaller.
   Ⓑ Animal plankton are more important.
   Ⓒ Animal plankton can move on their own.
   Ⓓ Plant plankton live in lakes, while animal plankton live in oceans.

6. Read the sentence from the article.

   > One reason is that plant plankton produces oxygen, just as green plants do on land.

   What does the word *produces* mean in this sentence?

   Ⓕ uses
   Ⓖ makes
   Ⓗ air and water
   Ⓘ fruits and vegetables

7. What would be the BEST reference source to learn more about plankton?

   Ⓐ an atlas
   Ⓑ an almanac
   Ⓒ an encyclopedia
   Ⓓ a social studies book

Reading Comprehension

GO ON

Read the story "Bringing Down the Moon" before answering Numbers 8 through 13.

Theme Test — Theme 6

Bringing Down the Moon

by Jonathan Emmett
Illustrations by Vanessa Cabban

"Hot diggety!" exclaimed Mole as he burrowed out of the ground one night. "Whatever's that?"

The moon was hanging in the sky above him like a bright silver coin. Mole thought that it was the most beautiful thing he had ever seen.

"Whatever it is, I must have it," Mole said to himself. "I know. I'll jump up and pull it down."

THUMP THUMP! THUMPETY BUMP!

Mole was so busy jumping he didn't think about the noise he was making, and he woke up Rabbit in her burrow.

"Mole!" said Rabbit. "What on earth do you think you're doing?"

"Hello, Rabbit," said Mole. "I'm trying to pull down that shiny thing."

"You mean the moon?" asked Rabbit.

"So that's what it's called," said Mole.

"You'll never do that," said Rabbit. "It's not as close as it looks."

But Mole would not give up. "I know," he thought. "I'll get a stick and poke it down." He found a long stick and poked it up at the moon.

SWISH SWISH! SWISHETY SWISH!

Mole was so busy poking that he tripped over Hedgehog in his bed of leaves.

"Mole," grunted Hedgehog. "What on earth are you up to?"

"Hello, Hedgehog," said Mole. "I'm trying to poke down the moon."

"You'll never do that," said Hedgehog. "It's not as close as it looks."

But Mole would not give up. "I know," he thought. "I'll throw something at it and knock it down." He found some acorns and threw them at the moon.

PLINK PLINK PLINKETY PLINK!

"Ouch!" said Squirrel. "Mole, have you gone nuts?"

"Hello, Squirrel," said Mole. "I'm trying to knock down the moon."

"You'll never do that," said Squirrel. "It's not as close as it looks."

But Mole wanted the moon so badly, he would not give up. "I know," he thought. "I'll climb a tree and carry it down!"

Mole had never climbed a tree before. It was hard work, and he was scared to be so far from the ground. But he kept on going until he saw the moon resting in the leaves above him.

Mole stretched out his paws. But just when he thought he had the moon . . . he slipped!

"Oh! Eeek! Ouch! Ooh!"

Mole tumbled down and landed SPLASH! in the middle of a puddle.

"Hot diggety" thought Mole. "I almost had it that time." Then he noticed something floating in the puddle beside him. It was pale and wrinkled, but Mole recognized it at once.

"The moon," whispered Mole. "It must have fallen down with me." He reached out to pick up the moon. But as soon as he touched it, it broke into pieces and vanished.

Mole sat in the puddle and cried. Rabbit, Hedgehog, and Squirrel came running up. "Are you all right, Mole?" asked Rabbit.

"I'm all right," sobbed Mole. "But the moon isn't! I pulled it down, and then I broke it, and it was SO beautiful . . . and now I'll never see it again."

"Oh, Mole," said Rabbit, "you couldn't have pulled down the moon."

"And you couldn't have broken it," said Hedgehog.

"And you'll certainly see it again," said Squirrel. "Look!"

High up in the sky above them, the moon was coming out from behind a cloud. "Oh," whispered Mole, "and it's just as beautiful as ever."

Mole, Rabbit, Hedgehog, and Squirrel stood and stared up at the moon together.

"It is beautiful," said Rabbit.
"Very beautiful!" said Hedgehog.
"Very beautiful indeed!" said Squirrel.
"Yes," said Mole. "But it's NOT as close as it looks!"

Name _____

Theme Test
Theme 6

▶ **Now answer Numbers 8 through 13. Base your answers on the story "Bringing Down the Moon."**

8. Which sentence from the story is an OPINION and not a fact?

    Ⓕ The moon was hanging in the sky above him, like a bright silver coin.

    Ⓖ Then he noticed something floating in the puddle beside him.

    Ⓗ Mole was so busy poking that he tripped over Hedgehog in his bed of leaves.

    Ⓘ Mole thought it was the most beautiful thing he had ever seen.

9. Which event happens FIRST?

    Ⓐ Mole climbs a tree to reach the moon.

    Ⓑ Mole tries to poke down the moon.

    Ⓒ Mole jumps to reach the moon.

    Ⓓ Mole tries to throw something at the moon.

10. Read the sentence from the story.

    "Mole, have you gone nuts?"

    What does the word *nuts* mean in this sentence?

    Ⓕ crazy

    Ⓖ smart

    Ⓗ something to eat

    Ⓘ a kind of stick used for poking

Reading Comprehension

GO ON

Name _____

Theme Test
Theme 6

11. Why does Mole think the moon is broken?

    Ⓐ Its reflection moves when he touches it.

    Ⓑ He finds pieces of it on the ground.

    Ⓒ He hears a loud sound when it falls.

    Ⓓ Rabbit tells him it had broken.

12. Which of the following words BEST describes Mole?

    Ⓕ mean

    Ⓖ sleepy

    Ⓗ grumpy

    Ⓘ curious

Name _____

Theme Test
Theme 6

13. What would have MOST LIKELY happened if Mole hadn't landed in the puddle? Use details and information from the story to support your answer.

_____
_____
_____
_____
_____
_____
_____
_____

Reading Comprehension

Name _____

▶ Read the article "The Daring Charles Lindbergh" before answering Numbers 14 through 20.

Theme Test
Theme 6

The Daring Charles Lindbergh

Amazing Airplanes

Today, no one thinks it is strange to travel long distances by airplane. However, when Charles Lindbergh became the first person to fly across the Atlantic Ocean in 1927, airplanes were still new. Some people had never even seen an airplane. But people loved the idea of flying. It was amazing to think about soaring like a bird. For those who flew, it was incredible to be able to see familiar objects such as houses and cars from the airplane. They looked as small as toys.

Lindbergh's Flight

There was a $25,000 prize for the first pilot who made it across the Atlantic Ocean without stopping. Lindbergh had been a pilot for years when he decided that he would enter that contest. He loaded his plane with huge tanks of gas. For himself, he had a quart of water and five sandwiches. Lindbergh set out from Long Island on May 20, 1927 as night was falling. He had no radio, so there was no way to know if he was safe.

Reading Comprehension

Lindbergh's Landing

Sixteen hours into the flight, he was already so tired that he had to hold his eyes open with his fingers. Lindbergh finally touched down on a landing field in Paris after 33-1/2 hours. One hundred thousand people had been waiting to see whether he would make it. He succeeded. They rushed forward to greet him. He set out as a pilot, and he landed as a hero.

Name _____

Theme Test
Theme 6

▶ **Now answer Numbers 14 through 20. Base your answers on the article "The Daring Charles Lindbergh."**

14. Why did the author write "The Daring Charles Lindbergh"?
    - Ⓐ to warn readers about airplane travel
    - Ⓑ to convince readers to become pilots
    - Ⓒ to tell about an interesting person
    - Ⓓ to explain how an airplane works

15. Why does the author say that Lindbergh "set out as a pilot" but "landed as a hero?"
    - Ⓕ Lindbergh would never be a pilot again after the flight.
    - Ⓖ Lindbergh's success made him famous and popular.
    - Ⓗ Lindbergh wanted to change his name.
    - Ⓘ Lindbergh was not a good pilot.

16. How would the same trip today compare to Lindbergh's flight?
    - Ⓐ It would be a shorter distance.
    - Ⓑ It would get more attention.
    - Ⓒ It would not be possible.
    - Ⓓ It would be faster.

Reading Comprehension

GO ON

Name _____

Theme Test
Theme 6

17. Read the sentence from the article.

> **Lindbergh set out from Long Island on May 20, 1927 as night was falling.**

What does the word *falling* mean in this sentence?
- Ⓕ dropping
- Ⓖ ending
- Ⓗ moving
- Ⓘ approaching

18. Which of the words below is a homograph?
- Ⓐ red
- Ⓑ dog
- Ⓒ close
- Ⓓ Lindbergh

19. Which of the words below is a homograph?
- Ⓕ read
- Ⓖ flight
- Ⓗ Paris
- Ⓘ airplane

Reading Comprehension   15   GO ON

Name _____

Theme Test
Theme 6

20. Write about Charles Lindbergh's important flight. Why was it so important? How does the author help you understand how important the flight was? Use details and information from the story to explain your answer.

Reading Comprehension

Name _____

Phonics/Spelling

Theme Test
Theme 6

▶ For Numbers 21 through 23, read each sentence that has a blank in it where a word is missing. Choose the word that has the same sound as the underlined part of the model word and that also completes the sentence.

21. na<u>tion</u>
    Did I _____ that I won first prize?
    Ⓐ say
    Ⓑ station
    Ⓒ explain
    Ⓓ mention

22. ses<u>sion</u>
    How good is your _____?
    Ⓕ sight
    Ⓖ vision
    Ⓗ hearing
    Ⓘ lesson

23. cau<u>tion</u>
    The book was full of _____.
    Ⓐ jokes
    Ⓑ portion
    Ⓒ stories
    Ⓓ fiction

Phonics/Spelling

GO ON

Name _____

Theme Test
Theme 6

▶ For Numbers 24 through 35, read the sentence that has a blank in it where a word is missing. Choose the correct form of the word to complete the sentence.

24. The poor baby bird was _____.
   - Ⓕ helpable
   - Ⓖ helpful
   - Ⓗ helpless
   - Ⓘ helpous

25. The friendly young man was very _____.
   - Ⓐ likable
   - Ⓑ likible
   - Ⓒ likeless
   - Ⓓ likeous

26. The rubber band was very _____.
   - Ⓕ flexable
   - Ⓖ flexible
   - Ⓗ flexful
   - Ⓘ flexeous

27. Playing with matches is very _____.
   - Ⓐ dangerable
   - Ⓑ dangerful
   - Ⓒ dangerless
   - Ⓓ dangerous

Phonics/Spelling

GO ON

Name _____

Theme Test
Theme 6

28. He brought his _____ to my house.
- (F) bicycle
- (G) surcycle
- (H) noncycle
- (I) overcycle

29. The silly story was full of _____.
- (A) bisense
- (B) sursense
- (C) nonsense
- (D) oversense

30. He used a bucket to catch the _____.
- (F) biflow
- (G) surflow
- (H) nonflow
- (I) overflow

31. I got _____ before speaking in front of the class.
- (A) nervable
- (B) nervible
- (C) nerveless
- (D) nervous

32. What is the first syllable of create?
- (F) cr
- (G) cre
- (H) crea
- (I) creat

Phonics/Spelling

GO ON

Name _____

Theme Test
Theme 6

33. What is the last syllable of ruin?
    - Ⓐ n
    - Ⓑ in
    - Ⓒ uin
    - Ⓓ ruin

34. What is the first syllable of violet?
    - Ⓕ v
    - Ⓖ vi
    - Ⓗ vio
    - Ⓘ viol

35. What is the last syllable of museum?
    - Ⓐ m
    - Ⓑ um
    - Ⓒ eum
    - Ⓓ seum

Phonics/Spelling
20
STOP

Name _____

Robust Vocabulary

Theme Test
Theme 6

▶ Choose the best word to complete each sentence for Numbers 36 through 45.

36. When the wind hit it, the boat began to _____.
    - (F) sway
    - (G) occur
    - (H) oblige
    - (I) expand

37. Will you _____ that I have the right number?
    - (A) remark
    - (B) confirm
    - (C) magnify
    - (D) elaborate

38. The tall mountain was beautiful and _____.
    - (F) aligned
    - (G) infinite
    - (H) inventive
    - (I) picturesque

39. John is too proud of himself; he is always _____.
    - (A) inviting
    - (B) bristling
    - (C) boasting
    - (D) summoning

Robust Vocabulary

GO ON

Name _____

Theme Test
Theme 6

40. When Henry plays tricks, he really makes a _____ of himself.
- Ⓕ gimmick
- Ⓖ nuisance
- Ⓗ magnify
- Ⓘ preparation

41. The water in the little creek was very _____.
- Ⓐ social
- Ⓑ shallow
- Ⓒ expansive
- Ⓓ uncharted

42. Watch the way the toy top _____ around.
- Ⓕ appears
- Ⓖ rotates
- Ⓗ reflects
- Ⓘ generates

43. Because she forgot to study, failing the test seemed _____.
- Ⓐ steady
- Ⓑ distinct
- Ⓒ adamant
- Ⓓ inevitable

Robust Vocabulary

© Harcourt • Grade 3

GO ON

44. He paid careful attention to his work; he was very _____.
    - F grainy
    - G thorough
    - H loyal
    - I dreadful

45. To solve the mystery, we looked at the _____.
    - A prey
    - B safeguard
    - C spiral
    - D evidence

Name _____

Grammar

Theme Test
Theme 6

▶ **Read and answer Numbers 46 through 55.**

46. Which of the following is an irregular verb?

    Ⓕ be
    Ⓖ hop
    Ⓗ toss
    Ⓘ jump

47. Which sentence is written correctly?

    Ⓐ He had begun his work.
    Ⓑ The dog had bited him.
    Ⓒ The car had breaked down.
    Ⓓ She had buyed new shoes.

48. Which sentence is written correctly?

    Ⓕ I seen it happen.
    Ⓖ She threw the ball.
    Ⓗ Has she took the test?
    Ⓘ Has he wrote his paper?

49. Which sentence is written correctly?

    Ⓐ He ran quick.
    Ⓑ He sat quiet.
    Ⓒ She walked slow.
    Ⓓ She skipped happily.

Grammar

Name _____

Theme Test
Theme 6

50. Which of the following does the adverb here describe?
    F) how
    G) why
    H) when
    I) where

51. Which shows the correct way to write the title of a book?
    A) The Little Red Hen
    B) The Little Red Hen
    C) "The Little Red Hen"
    D) "The Little Red Hen"

52. Which of the following is a negative verb contraction?
    F) it's
    G) she's
    H) aren't
    I) where'll

53. Which sentence is written correctly?
    A) I can't come.
    B) We won't not go.
    C) He didn't not understand.
    D) He does not have no books.

Grammar

GO ON

Name _____

Theme Test
Theme 6

54. In which sentence is all of the punctuation correct?
    Ⓕ I like corn carrots and peas.
    Ⓖ I saw Mary, Sam, and Charles.
    Ⓗ Carter ate ham and he liked it.
    Ⓘ Sally ran fast and Harry did too.

55. Which sentence is written correctly?
    Ⓐ Did you ask doctor Brown?
    Ⓑ He asked mrs. Smith to come.
    Ⓒ I hope Mr. Miller can make it.
    Ⓓ Please invite the man from alaska.

Grammar

Name _____

Writing to a Prompt

Theme Test
Theme 6

Exploring the Arctic

In the early 1900s, a race began to reach the North Pole. Many people had tried and failed before. The North Pole is the center of the Arctic Circle and is surrounded by water and ice. In fact, the North Pole isn't even on land. It was almost impossible for anyone to reach it.

In 1909, Robert Peary and Matthew Henson claimed to be the first humans to reach the North Pole. Their guides, four people who lived near the Arctic Circle, traveled with them. This was the end of years of hard work.

Peary and Henson traveled many miles over the frozen Arctic Ocean. They learned to drive dog sleds over the ice and snow. They carried extra clothing, medicine, and food in the dog sleds. They had to wear special clothes so they didn't freeze. Peary and Henson could not do it alone. They had a team of more than twenty people helping them along their way. On April 6, 1909, Peary and Henson reached their goal. They were the first people to reach the pole, or so they thought.

When Peary and Henson came home, they were in for a surprise. Another man, Frederick Cook, said he had reached the North Pole before them. After an investigation, the world decided that Peary and Henson were the first to reach the North Pole. The debate may never end. Today, some scientists have suggested that neither Peary nor Cook really reached the North Pole.

Writing to a Prompt

GO ON

Explore the Arctic

Come see the beautiful Arctic. Let our guides show you some of the amazing wildlife here. The memories will last forever.

Sign up today for our July trip:

July 2–29

The Animals You Will See:

Polar bears are one of the largest bears on earth. They have thick, oily, white fur. Their fur protects them when they swim in icy water.

On land, their large feet act like snowshoes. They don't sink into the snow. The hair on the bottom of their feet helps them walk without slipping on ice.

Arctic foxes are about the same size as a cat. They have short legs, short ears, and a long, bushy tail.

During the summer, their fur is grayish brown. It turns white in the winter, so the foxes are hard to see in the snow. Like polar bears, foxes have hair on the bottom of their feet so they don't slip on ice.

The Plants You Will See:

Saxifrage is a plant that can grow between rocks. Its name means rock-breaker. The leaves grow in a cluster at the bottom of the plant. The flowers can be different colors. There are about 300 species of this plant.

Mountain avens is also a flowering plant. It is part of the rose family. The plants generally have yellow or white flowers. They grow on ledges and rocky slopes.

The **Arctic Iceland poppy** has white, orange, or red flowers. The flowers last a long time. They have a strong scent.

Writing to a Prompt

Dear Logan,

    I just arrived at the research site. It is just inside the Arctic Circle. Remember how I showed you where I was going on the map? The North Pole is the center of all the land and water found inside the Arctic Circle. The Arctic Circle is the area around the North Pole. It is made up of islands, the Arctic Ocean, and the northern areas of several countries.

    I'm glad that I came in the summertime when it is warmer. Did I tell you that the sun hardly sets in the summer? There is even one day every summer when the sun never sets at all. In the winter, the opposite happens. The night lasts longer. Again, there is a day where the sun never comes up. When the sun does come up, it doesn't stay up very long.

    I'll be sure to write more soon.

                              Love,
                              Aunt Lori

Name _____

Arctic Circle Fast Facts

Theme Test
Theme 6

Fact 1
Several countries have land inside the Arctic Circle:
Canada, Denmark, Norway, Sweden,
Finland, Russia, the United States, and Iceland.

Fact 2
Greenland, the largest island in the world, is
almost completely inside the Arctic Circle.

Writing to a Prompt

Name _____

Theme Test
Theme 6

> The Arctic Cirle is an interesting region to explore.
> Think about what you learned about the Arctic.
> Now write a report about what you learned about the Arctic.

Planning Page

▶ Use this space to make your notes before you begin writing.
The writing on this page will NOT be scored.

_____
_____
_____
_____
_____
_____
_____
_____
_____
_____

Writing to a Prompt

Name _____

**Theme Test
Theme 6**

▶ **Begin writing here. The writing on this page and the next WILL be scored.**

Writing to a Prompt

Name _____

Theme Test
Theme 6

Writing to a Prompt

Name _____

Theme Test
Theme 6

Oral Reading Fluency

Katie Clare is a nine-year-old detective. She solves mysteries that are very old. How does she do it?

Katie is a fossil collector, or "rock hound." Almost every weekend, Katie and her parents go fossil hunting.

Katie has never found a dinosaur fossil. The fossils she finds are just as interesting, though. When she finds one, Katie carefully chips at the rock around it with her hammer. Once the fossil is out, she wraps it carefully in newspaper. Then she puts it in her bag. Some of the things Katie finds are too difficult to collect. They might be damaged if she tried to remove them from the rock. Katie places soft paper over the rock and then rubs charcoal on the paper to make a picture of the leaf or shell that is buried in the rock.

When Katie gets home, she takes out her fossils and her rubbings. She uses her fossil book to look up the names and ages of her plant and animal fossils. Then she sorts the rocks carefully into little boxes. These boxes make up her collection.

Name _____

Theme Test
Theme 6

Have you ever had an idea for a new invention? People are always coming up with new ideas, but very few people have the skill to make their inventions. That is why Beulah Henry is so special.

Beulah Henry was born in 1887. She is known to have had 49 inventions during her life. Some people believe she had ideas for more than 100 inventions.

Many of Beulah Henry's inventions were for children. She invented a kind of sponge that made bath time more fun. She also invented learning games.

Beulah Henry came up with many inventions to make housework easier. She made new kinds of sewing machines and a new kind of can opener.

The best known of Beulah Henry's inventions was a new kind of umbrella. It was made with snaps. People could snap different colored fabrics onto the umbrella to match their clothing. Many people wanted to buy these umbrellas. They were sold all over the country.

Beulah Henry died in 1973. In her long life, she came up with more inventions than almost any other inventor of her time.

Oral Reading Fluency

STOP

STORYtown
HARCOURT SCHOOL PUBLISHERS

Discoveries/Theme 6

Grade 3

Theme Tests

www.harcourtschool.com

ISBN-13: 978-0-15-368492-0
ISBN-10: 0-15-368492-5

Part No. 9997-87105-7 (Package of 12) 3-2